T0323981

SAVING WATER

Allan Kolski Horwitz

First published by Botsotso Publishing
Box 30952, Braamfontein, 2017, South Africa
Email: botsotso@artslink.co.za

Poems © Allan Kolski Horwitz

ISBN: 0-620-35444-5

Many of these poems (in the current or earlier versions) have previously appeared in the
following magazines/anthologies/collections/websites: Bliksem, Botsotso, Cambridge
Poetry Review, Carapace, Donga, Dirty Washing, Fidelities, Green Dragon, Greetings
Emsawawa, The Heart in Exile, Illuminations, Il Vascello di Carta, Kotaz, Leaves to a
Tree, Litnet, New Coin, Purple Light Mirror in the Mud, Rattapallax, Staffrider,
Southern Rain, Timbila, Throbbing Ink, We Jive like This

The poet wishes to thank the National Arts Council of South Africa for their support.

NATIONAL ARTS COUNCIL
OF SOUTH AFRICA

Cover & text design and layout: Anna Anuradhá Varney
Cover drawing: Allan Kolski Horwitz

CONTENTS

THE BRIDE

She is the bride of allah
The bride of jesus
She is the bride of elohim the king of hosts
Of rocks and temples

She is the bride of a man who does not appreciate her; he ignores her
She is the bride of a man who honours her; he smiles with respect

She is the bride of a man who loves and desires her; he treasures her
beauty
She is the bride of a man who defiles her; he claims she wants to be raped

She is the bride of a man who adores her but is impotent; he buys her gifts
She is the bride of a man who deserts her; he is a serial philanderer

She is the bride of a man who wills her to die; he is disturbed by her
power
She is the bride of a man who makes her bear child after child; he sees her
as expanding his influence

She is the bride of a man who shares the household duties; he is cheerful
She is the bride of a man who will not let her work outside of the house;
he is fearful of her independence

She is the bride of a man who supports her; he is generous
She is the bride of a man who belittles her: he is hunched and unsure with
other men

She is the bride of a man who kisses her and holds her hand in the street
She is the bride of a man who slaps her in front of her family
She is the bride of a man who brings her to joyful conception
She is the bride of a man who forces himself on her without warning

She is the bride of allah
The bride of elohim
The bride of krishna
She is the bride of jesus

She is my bride and I will try to defy the gods

JACARANDA, BLUE AND PURPLE CARPET

Fleur in the sky
at the level of trees
the level of eyes
open to the blue world beyond sight
beyond imagining
-mother of all nothingness
and muchness

blue-blue
in which we do
not find reflection
blue-blue absorbs
the birds and bees
who do as they please

especially

when jacaranda weds jillaranda
and they kiss purple

violet petals

I drive down these streets
summer breeze
blessing the hands that planted
these trees

-rhapsody in jacaranda/jillaranda time

VOYAGER

He is on the road
The trip will take several hours
The landscape will change
The light will change
He will listen to music
He will receive phone calls
He will make phone calls
He will receive and send sms's

He will meditate on his life:

Women
Children
Work
Social games
Procedures
Flirtations
Political brutalities
Art

Art
Art

He phones his love once more to tell her
He wants to feel her lips on his lips
His hands on her hips
Hands on her woman's hips
Feel the skin slide
The hand glide

He is on the road

They laugh together and are warm

THE RHYTHM OF CREATION PERFECTS

Flock of white birds
One waving darting bird

Flight
A flock of one

Bird
A flowing of white birds

LITTLE PEOPLE, BIG PEOPLE
Salmanslaagte, Cedarberg

On either side of the river
  along ledges
little people mix roots and stone
 ochre
  painting
themselves
        and the animals that flee
  and feed
(flee from the arrow of their destiny
  -animals who keep the little people strong

they make fire on the ledges when the moon rises
  they admire their work while they dance
    the moon rises   fire glows

  the little people inscribe lips
all their lives joining to give mouth
to the traveller who comes in another time
  to the river
past plantations of rooibos in rows along the back of the kloof

  the little people

hunted
captured
fed drink and disease
   by the big people

        become
white winged eagles
  circling the kloof
eagles come to vouch for the spirits of the little people
      and the black ribbed lizard pulsing on rock

*

black ribbed lizard testifies
  beyond

the big people
the little people

all

seeking to pay tribute
  make peace

beyond vast cities
 beyond arsenals
   beyond property

our needing more than we need

*

the visitor in another time steps forward
  snake darts brown in the dry bush
    just a fl ash
before boots
prepare to
  join the little people's
    dance

  moondancefiredanceeagledanceochredancelivingspiritkloof

    living with what is around us

XMAS DAY: TWO DEATHS AND A RACIST

News comes by telephone:

Nomonde has died -
diabetic with high blood pressure
son stepping out of circumcision school
when she complained
taken to hospital
now her family are phoning for funeral money
which we cannot give
Mafuta   the manager who couldn't manage
replaced weeks ago
by someone called Hope

another call:

Enian, the Mad Turk
smothered in Table Bay by a cargo
of gypsum
Enian dead at the docks
trapped in a hold
of whom a story was told:
arrived one Xmas at a farm
near Richmond dressed as Santa Claus
though the host disliked him
was accepted by a blonde woman
-came with gifts for all
the Christian girls

then there's John the Forgetful on the line:

Barry Bent, the consultant
cooked on English moors and their pudding
small business expert
has got another plan
got it all down
talks dirty about kaffirs
but willing
to civilize them at a price
oh lord bleeding jesu
but we do need his advice

that's the day

EMPTY BELLIES TREMBLE

Bellies tremble and
with hungering fingers

take out knives (such hope
-lessness) waiting for night
for cloud, for quiet and sleeping sentries
we wait to fill ourselves
a little

may the snouts of sniffer dogs
ignore our pad

this night which covers sentries
whose cocked revolvers wake to jam us
at the windows – thin frames too thick
for larceny

we walk

filling shacktowns   new planets
with our loot   our staples   our dream-machines

we shack-dwellers of the end zones
take the last bus to zones
of plenty of green   of sharp fanged dogs

passing trees and flower beds
deep freezers stocked with meat and fish
passing the walls of these mansions
wise and worthy millionaires whose children
howl and hoot

passing all these things

we who have
  next to nothing
    except
the throttled air of hungering

take out our knives (such hope
-lessness

KAREEDOUW ROAD

I hear with my little ear,
something beginning with . . .

  b-s'

in the wheat fields and the green/yellow trees by the road –
      'birdsong'

*

a lone bird
sits on a telephone wire
a lone man sits in a car
he wants to write down ideas in his book

a boy plays by a tree
with a porcupine quill
found in the misty forests

he sticks the quill
into the bark of the green/yellow leafed tree
sticks it hard into the bark
-hard as he can

*

the man writes what he sees
    feels

the boy jumps into the car
    says:

  do you want to kill me?

*

they love each other
but sometimes
the man wants to write
and the boy wants to play

*

the birds gathered on the wire
sing

they sing for the man in the car
the boy on the ground
they sing when a truck roars past

the birds sing and the man writes
the boy sticks the porcupine quill
into the bark
the man sticks the pen into his mind

THE STREET AND THE SINGLE SORROW

The pulse of the street
   pulse of the single sorrow

  stabs of heart
crushed broken voices
burning aching voids
vulnerable to the appetites of others
not just their own

when blood of history and present carnage
seeps in to madden moments of blinding life

 I tremble
     from time to

 this time

 *

late morning
blossoms fall
a piano plays its cadence
soft feet and counter time
   I am at my round table
   with its inlaid spiral

  I write:

  Love is

It must matter

   It must matter that we act

ALL

The warthog the butterfly
the waterhole the muddy brown bird
the naartjie the man spitting pips
the hemp bush
the green snake

quiet midday waves
humming
drawing
all together

*

The ocean the beach
the dune the headland
the scrub the lighthouse
the moonlight

hushing and drawing

together

*

You
woman
are the first and last curve
of light and stone and wave
as you lift your arms to the moon
and the sand on your thighs
dusts itself off

you are smoothness as flesh
and spirit is your breath
in the water
breath is your mouth
drawing me into your centre

altogether

all
together

NO TWO WAKINGS THE SAME

No two wakings the same
sweat-ridden or radiant
blue sky or rain
vague winds blowing in
through structural cracks
the dragon's flame never altogether
consuming

4 JULY 1999

Today in Port Alfred
I touched the dunes that lie
naked and fine
I ran sand through my fingers

In the parking lot
a man in a dirty overall
offered to wash my car
He was toothless and thin

I ate in a restaurant
facing the beach and the ocean
I watched waves swell and break
surfers crouch to ride that motion

I watched the waters roll
across the brilliance of the sun's reflection
the headland curve out of sight
spray strike the jetty

I paid for my breakfast
walked back to my car
I gave the man R10
and a leftover sausage

AT BHEKAPANSI PAN

Very still and quiet
                in the heat

we (humans) coming in
on the dirt track
busy spotting
  animals birds   insects

when the sun passes its zenith
mud pools glisten
two warthogs approach

day shows we can climb
into

    it

a brown bird with long legs
    black beak
bathes in the water   flapping

warthog rolls in the mud
grunts
turns on its back   snorting

I feel you beside me and want
to push and coast
your flesh through your pants
 the curving crack
  shiver with the tingling
bells of your bum

the warthog rolls
 brown bird flaps
I run my fingers up
and

    down

you touch my leg
  we press together
-drunken edge

of joy-
soft and hard
excite

brown bird hops to the side of the mud
pool
you see a green snake slide over
a dead branch

we stop

green snake with a small rodent in its mouth
a long blade of grass

I press deeper
you stroke my tip
till it slides

dry stillness of the waterhole
flapping brown bird wings
warthog farts   rolls out the mud
rubs up against
the rough bark of a thorn tree
green snake wriggles
into the undergrowth

  sweet love

    out of time

bhekapansi
   the old time comes

-look and be joined

FROM THE TIPS OF BLACKENED BRANCHES

Fire

ac r os s the   s l o
                       pe
                            s

   under

     over
     hangs

    bet
   ween
    cr e
    vic
     e
    s

devouring shoots and branches
    grass and flowers
 f ire blistering the mountain
 squeezing juice
into hard balls
of sooty charcoal

     protea trees
inky   bare   gnarled
branch tangles to show the traveller
burnt   (loss   disdain)
blackened arms lifting
to the light

 at each tip
   glowing

  a green child

IN MEMORIAM: MOLELEKWA, KERKORREL

Yes, dead brothers

afternoon rain clearing the city
I mourn you

make a mark
  keep memory
          alive

the musics you made
coming out of and   into time
  stay

free   despite the mocking mad cymbals
that came and drowned
(you tried to be free with the sound
 the notes of your last hours
black water rising as the outburst
 broke banks
-hands thundered
 that made so much beauty
so much pain turn into sadness

hanged

  brothers
          I am split

take my tempo
recompose me
untie your notes from the ropes
so your music plays

and plays

  and plays

DANGER: NIGHT BATHING PROHIBITED

When the black waters
release spray into the black night
and the black feet of night
submerge in the black waters

do not swim
do not allow the current to suck you
back to the source of the spring
do not swim at night
those black waters will suck you
under!

the sign is clear: night bathing prohibited
so
find a quiet place
far from the glare of lights
keep a quiet moment
let the stars blink
for suns must flare
then steady your pulse
and dive

do not close your eyes!
with salt stinging
  swim

       with sand gritting
     light slipping

swim with open eyes

   wave swelling
    shark slicing
    tide sucking

swim with eyes wide enough
to open the night

stars burning in the soundless distance
as you swim
in the before-everything

before and after
everything

remember: dreams which might lead to instability are prohibited
which might lead to aftershock
to insomnia
dreams which make it possible to say
nothing is impossible

remember: nothing except abuse is prohibited

so swim in the dark
sleep with your eyes wide open

bathing and dreaming

PHOTOGRAPH OF A MAN IN BAGHDAD

The father holds his dead son in his arms
the camera clicks and his grief is able to
cover the whole world and history

the father is holding his dead son
because
an American armed personnel carrier moments earlier
was blown up by a suicide bomber

the father is holding his murdered son
because
the Americans who invaded Iraq to free the people of their vicious dictator
throw chocolates for children from armed personnel carriers

the father has been photographed holding his murdered son
because
the Americans destroyed as much as they liberated
and again fascists challenge for power

the father holds his dead son
and I imagine holding my son
bloody and breathless
my precious son
all bloody and breathless
and I cry
with the father in Baghdad
whose son chased chocolates thrown from armed personnel carriers
bags of sweets for twenty other children whose fathers
now carry spattered with iron fragments
and the flesh of the suicide bomber

the father's tears fall onto his son
fall onto me holding my son in my arms
the father's tears fall and I kiss my son and then
let him run out to play
while I look at the man in Baghdad
and wonder about the funeral

I watch my son play in the garden
and wonder how the father in Baghdad is managing to go about
his life

then I call to my son
I hold him and kiss him again
and again

I want to protect him from
the sweets of human madness

THE WALL HAS FALLEN
October, 1989 – For Bertold Brecht

Comrades

> the berlin Wall has fallen to the trumpets
of profit making
>> profit taking
>>> profit raking

the Wall has fallen to the trumpets of seduction

> rotted bricks and concrete
rotted commissars and custodians

jail Wall

and those comrades who needed
to build such a Wall
now need to come out of the debris of the Wall
and dust off

dust vision

Wall smeared with blood instead of paint across
the human length and breadth
Wall blinded those in front of it
those behind it

those who patrolled it
those who surveyed it
those who crossed over at the checkpoints

and those who were stopped

but now the Wall   comrades   has fallen

> these bricks

what are we now going to try and build with these bricks?

VIBRATIONS

What is this restlessness?

what is the root of the restlessness
the wand root like
quivering in search of the quarry
the wandering quarry

the wand quivering with senses
wanting the wind to bring
perfumes

why this restlessness?
this alertness
    this seeking to be thrilled
to make sharp and taste

why this need for keener vibrations?

FESTIVAL

"The sight of your eyes . . .
tresses . . .
when you smile your lips curve . . .
olive skin glowing . . .
your warm hand . . .
laughter's firm breasts . . ."

he does not wish to be imperious
insists
he does not wish to be silly
this sort of magic
should not make him mawkish
nor moody nor sloppy

just make him sing
the radiant dance of her brownness

KWESCHINS 4 WURLD INSANITEE DAY

wy ar theire stil hungree homeliss chilldrin
in th streeetsz

wy are theire old pippel stil shvering coz thay dont
hav monee 4 elektrsitee

wy hav wee mest up th ozonn

wy arnt the guvermint pippel onist

wy do wee kneed so menee drugz

wy do wee ned 2 step on antsz

wy doo sum pippel hav so mutch munee

wy doo sum pippel need so mutch munee

whi doo sume pippel luv dogz and catsz mor than thay luv
uthur pipple

whi iz thair sutch a thing az butee

wy doo wee dy

all2gethair chilldrin:
say thank yu 4 butee
say thank yu 4 luv
thank god 4 thinking ov us
luv god
lieke yorself
doo good
doo wot yu kan

REAGANOMICS

Years of fireside television
chats about titanic evil
-the Soviet Satan and Nicaraguan peasants
years of junk bonds escalating
garbage and junk sludging the oil-refineries of New Jersey
fists of white powder jamming the toilets of the stock-exchange
stretch-limousines glistening like hearses in light rain on Park
Avenue . . .

how New York loved itself!
Capital of Kapital and clubs
with shades and silver sky-mirrors shrieking:
I am the fairest of them all,
State of the Art

you kept us in thrall
(and the wretched rat in the alley behind a Chinese restaurant
 behind a health-store and the doorman's shadow)
subways sagging at night
lines hurtling to Brooklyn the Bronx
lines of coke lurching to Queen's
phantoms riding an escalator from the periphery to this centre
of the American pulse -
        O, Babylon

long nights cruising your grid
a rider disdaining dollars
seduced by madonnas therapists telephone-sex operators
        I remember you exploding
        with hot hemp in a circle of jive
        sweet and sour dreams
        of roller skating fiends
        and priests of the ghettoes
        balmers of ragged spirits
        offering doves voodoo and salsa

Big Apple
all rosy with the saliva of hookers
    you dared us to throng

you shouted down Broadway
come with the scroll of your names
come gasp

I would traverse you on hire
at ease at the ready to drive and be driven
sharp to the knife the kiss
the amphetamine in your party hours
leather boys sticky with darkrooms
disco kids in cutaway T-shirts
5am on 8th Avenue whistling for rides

how you would glow in the night

   rising

    Atlantis!

till faint tinge of dawn silvering the river
banks of the Hudson waking with springing lights
aggrandizement of pleasure
clawing the world as their domain for plunder
almost ignorant of the reality of feeling
the dialectic of challenge

   I would follow
  connecting the glass surface of calm
those cliffs of New Jersey
saluting their architects
towers suspended above the water

I would almost forget
those lights springing across the river
were people rising for work

GRAHAMSTOWN BAND

In the cold season sun strains behind cloud
man in a crowd hoists his child
musicians on stage play their instruments and sing
about the train that used to take
black men from the north down south
to dig gold for white men
that train whistling like the draught in tunnels
before gas explodes and rock crumbles

clouds drift
sun catches the man and the child on his shoulders
today
the whistle is not that of wind on bleached bone
brought up from the bowels of white ridges
but a flute surging across the dome of a mouth

the child in the swaying crowd
turns to face the star his father praises as the source of life
the one amongst many which is everything
so not even underground lives can be eternally squashed

all sway to this sun music in the cold season
they all sway: stimela

BLACK AND RED VENUS

black venus
  coy khoi

        eyes and breasts
            joyful curls

nevermind the bouncers' bruises
on your a-starte-ling body
   we fit
and nothing and no one
can take that away
  from us

nevermind your lilting cracked smile
your halting street language
 we fit
and nothing and no one can take that
     away
         from us

nevermind the passing cars
the mobile surfing ocean drowning
our sighs and moans
   frenzied fingers tangled
   with salt   with weed

                nevermind

  we fit
O gariep venus
     we fit!

nothing and no one can take that away
      from
          us

THE BIRDS AT MY WINDOW

There are two birds at my window
one of wood, one of stone

green stone of the rocks by the river
shone to shine with its depths
hard wood that grows in the mountain earth
scented with wind and dust and rain

the birds at my window
sing

day and night

by day they sing of adventure and war
and scientific invention
by night they sing of birth and death
the springs of joy and convulsion

the birds at my window
perch without moving
their wings do not lift
their beaks do not tremble

the birds at my window sing
inside me

DURING THE DROUGHT

Dreaming of frogs
in a dry house
no rain comes through the holes
in the roof

dreaming of frogs
one becomes hundreds! they're all over the place!

she fears sleep
(who can taste rest with frogs
squatting on your breasts, your stomach,
 your mouth. . . ?

she fears sleep
soon her eyes become blackened empty wells
blue rings fill her sockets
her hands drop to her sides

she cannot sleep

she visits the healer

the healer dances
opens her mouth and blows out the green scaly spirits
pours in dew tapped in a forest
the healer binds a monkey tail round her waist
anoints her with ash

soon she will jump from dream to dream
without flinching
leathery thong round her waist

wear it till the frogs return to their swamp
wear it till the turning earth lulls her to sleep
wear it close round her thighs

the healer binds her with a thong
now she sleeps
and dreams of me
her husband
seeding her
with a circle of round sweet faces

I am her prince

FIRST

we support his coup - the elected government seems to be tilting towards another power

then

we train his militias - there are terrorists in the south, a militant underground

then

we endorse his banning political parties and declaring martial law in the north - there's trouble with another faction

then

we support his dissolving parliament, firing the judges and heads of the civil service appointed by the elected government

then

we give him the go-ahead to outlaw the trade unions - secret cabals working for our corporate rivals

then

we ship in specialists to train his secret police - information gathering equipment that doesn't leave marks

then

we loan him our latest surveillance technology to record the corners of every street

then

we loan him billions to buy the deadliest systems – smart bombs, smart bacteria

then

we applaud his silencing the independent media to counter their shameless propaganda against the war we want him to fight then

we give him the green light to liberate a neighbouring country and control access to regional production

then

we let the generals in his army dominate the drug trade and launder their profits to finance other clandestine operations

then

we sign further contracts with him to develop the mines in the east and deposit the money we pay him into our banks

then

we sell him prime land in our capital to build a luxurious embassy and attend state banquets as an honoured guest

then

we give him medals, make him a doctor of philosophy at our most prestigious university

then

we nominate him chair of the UN Human Rights Committee and lean on ninety countries

then

we watch him swell and puff and dance to the tune of an orchestra heard in his head alone

then

we have to blockade him
shock and awe with our killing machines
till only our song again takes the air
only our song fills the tv stations in his palaces and barracks

and then . . .

   we replace him with his son

RANK ROSE

Beautiful vagina
at the end of which the sacred lake
purifies

full of fecund darkness
sweet and sour sperm
seeking combination

rough perfume and silky slide
cradle and grave for all men
flesh sons and procreating daughters

beautiful vagina
has taken ten thousand years
to form her lips and speak her glories

beautiful warm vagina
makes me sing the songs
of ten thousand years of rocking

joyous song that rises
from the ebb and flow of skin
singing blind

wet warm vagina
welcoming
each primal action

BLACK MUD

Hey, black mud

  out of you comes the white lily
  out of you comes the water flame

  and from your ooze come vibrations turning air into sand, sand
into crystal

black mud

  from your lips come rough roars and kisses
  from your womb come hot phrases and cutting edges turning baby
bouncy blue and pulse

perfect

black mud

  how do you and the drum say it?
  how do you and the sax play it?

black mud

  toes digging your bed of beat
  heart is an ivory ripple
  hot and cool like a drunkard's drool
  at a hooker's nipple

you got it, black mud, you got it

  out of you comes the white lily
  out of you comes the water flame

SPRING RAIN

Oak leaves in one week
greedy out the dormant stem
break through old winter bark
tender eyes opening
pushing into the dusty air

I stand in front of my door
children behind me
and look forward to the season of acorns -
they will grow
then fall to the ground for us to collect

During the first rainstorm
lightning cuts and crackles
thunder bombards the sky that claps back
dogs bark and whimper
scrape at the door wanting to hide under the beds
the tree is covered with
little fingers feeling and conducting the wind

rain crashes down the windows and the night
        dark and wet
    your buttocks   your breasts
        your hot tongue

it is good to be at home with you
my darling

06/01/02

Cacti and doringboom
make it to the top of the mountain
moss creeps over the rocks
little blue birds flit and trill
across the valley

far away
you cry to me –
a bad night   all the bloody
ghosts crawling

i love you
but you won't let me in
you choke
and my words evaporate

a black butterfly with blue
circles on its wings
settles near me
and flutters while i
feel your absence

POWER

all power to the awakened people

may the despots tremble then flee

all power to the awakened people

may the robbers surrender their spoils

may the gangsters hide in fear of detention

all power to the awakened people

may the people keep clear of temptation and sloth
may the people remember the stories of their scars
may the people's leaders respect the people
may the people respect themselves and their leaders
may the air fill with the perfumes of a hundred flowers
may the people awaken from the restless sleep of blood

all power to the awakened people

all power to all people

ROOTS

From the neat surface
thrusting into the dark
locus of water and mineral
thrusting through the drought
till the final withering

Beyond every surface
a surface

I SEE YOU AT THE FENCE

looking out at the river
the current that takes and lets float
then sinks us or throws us
to the bank where we rot in the sun
or crawl and find food or
plant and wait for edibles to grow and eat

I see you at the fence in a black robe
white hands touching your red hair
still pale from the northern clouds
you stagger about at a loss
hands that strangled or aborted
futures not found a safe and proper burial

you are brittle sensitive and quick
tense because the fish eagle soaring
in the thermals above the river
must still descend and clamp you
in its talons and take you up
where you cannot breathe but will come alive

I watch you while beyond the fence peasants weed their fields
sweat under the indifferent sun
you wish to give them your green fingers
water systems and modern sewerage
because you do not see me
you cannot wish to give me anything

BEFORE RESUMING WAR

Half-
 deeds misdeeds deedless
   happenings
 cross-deeds
  back-deeds   side-deeds
  cold-hot deeds
    icy   exact   snarling deeds

sink trained terrible teeth
bringing red and black to our eyes

they cut the lull and make us jump

*

We act according
to the sway of evening
the current
the threat of reefs
the image of our destination

*

Dawn

deep
restful
cold water

ETERNAL HONEY

Valley of lilies
high in the kloof
reed river runs
   leaves fall
upon the waters

Valley of lilies
black bank of soil
green cradling candle
   bee dangles
in a white cup

Valley of lilies
yellow stamen
gleaming fuzz
   striped husk
of silent buzzing

Valley of lilies
wine water womb
night angle sunshine
   worker sips
eternal honey

SURELY

Making love with eyes open
meeting the glare
of imperfection seeking
  perfection

  is wise

when the wave's curve and the wind's current
  entwine
surely love must unfurl

surely love must fly when eyes open
  surely love must fly
    and eyes open

surely love must fly with eyes

                wide   open

love's perfection   loving imperfection
        desire and affection
  is wise

AT LAST
Beyond genocide

Grey wind-lashed day
the photograph of your murdered sisters and brother
shrieking windward gulls
the photograph of us
three children in front of an orange tree
side by side
awkward joy and gentleness
before the eye of day
the camera

so many years:
this room your table
full with cards letters and scissors
books and tapes
mirror and the wooden clock

now on a tray
disposable needles
ampules
a nurse in white with a register

we wait with you
the final soundless hours
the morphine doing
what no one else
can do:
all we can do is surround you

HIGHVELD WINTER, LISTENING TO UM KALSUM

Stubble, birds peck at stalks
worms scrawl in blackened dust
writhe under stabbing beaks

orchestras in burnt gardens
birds split charred seeds
sirens vibrate behind a torn veil

voice of the blind sensualist
this woman with pears on her chest
a nightingale singing to sleep

VESSELS IN THE TEMPLE

They lie in the sun caked with residue
priests sucking their fingers
attendants in sweaty garments loitering near the gates
they greet passers-by with loud jeers and gestures

inside the Sanctuary tablets bleed
stained shattered broken feet of the Golden Father
in a yard under the leaves of a flowering mulberry tree
a young woman with glistening black hair
sings a lullaby to her child
song spilling out drumbeats
ecstatic pounding of feet

in another yard under the leaves of a flowering mulberry tree
a young woman with very black almost blue hair
sings of the fierceness of dogs in the desert
the cruel wrench of their jaws
the bitter nights spent fleeing
the strained days scanning horizons

both women rock their babies
toes touch the lips of a jar
spice from islands they can never reach
fragrant in the altar smoke
they tip the jars onto their feet
thick coat of red

there in the temple after the sacrifice
priests licking bones clean
mulberry trees spreading their juicy stain
the women rock their children

THE REWARDS OF CLIMBING

Start to climb, get into your stride

Face the rock
Feel the wind

And as you rise above the plain
Never look down on others

Never look down when you're climbing
Never look down to check how high you are
Keep climbing
Be respectful to others
Keep your gaze clear

And when you lift your eyes to the sun
To the stars
Do not tread on others
Keep the pace

Keep climbing

The peaks are elusive
Their slopes thick with thorns
Kloofs riven with tangles

Face the rock, feel the wind
Hear the creatures around you call out their natures

Keep climbing
The peaks will come into view
You will experience the peaks

Keep climbing

RARE

Above the swing of ocean current
specked with wood from unnamed ships
you are a rare bird beating rare air

I would have called to you
but the uneasiness of nearness of rawness
wantlessness prevailed
closing the half-apparent breach
teaching the unused moment
to retreat

and drawn towards the moon's full ring
where birds do not sing nor wing
nor rise before the current's wind
I cry bitter tears
live bitter fears

*

Your body a sheer cliff
the scent of
a vast undertaking

I have held a reed
at the base of your kloof
suppliant tenacious tuning the wind
brown long-stemmed slit
sometimes in dry earth sometimes in mud
I have brought you to my lips
to blow your veins with my rustling

*

There is no magic like your thigh
there is no spell like your ripened mouth

there is no magic like your sigh
there is no spell like your warm sheath

you are too gentle for my lumbering words
they engulf you like thundering storms

I am too blind for your protean eyes
they dazzle me like lightning mirrors

*

Once on a wind-swept day
the bed was firm
it did not creak
I loved you well
very deep
your small nipples
soft as fingers

*

Never such as you

above the swing of ocean current
skeined with wood from unsigned ships
rare bird
cresting waves of rare air

ANTENNAE FOR THE RACE

She defends him to the world
calls his well deep and sweet

she stands beside him
counts the way to one hundred
keeps the groove

he engine
of her joy
she the joy
of him

in the room they live
his wife with a sacred clasp
they dance in the cool\warm
days and nights
when there are breezes
they dance

light\dark pattering

AMSTERDAM: PHOTOGRAPHIC EXHIBITION

The Nile flows at Luxor
three robed boys at peace with sunset
drift beyond circumstance
the isolating frame cutting the hours after
the hours before
at ease with the current
whether the waters whirl with wind
whiten with fish
or throw up the marvel
of a corpse or
a queen

I stand beside them along canals
in this mercantile city
victims and lovers of the
Nile snake
since the time before names

COMPULSION

At night
expelled from a garden
to a red desert
cast under a moonless murkiness
become a trace in the dunes

she climbs to where
water in a slit rock boils
granite horizons gape with the lightning-blood
of a womb

and she remembers the green fields
far from the smoking of sulpher pools
volcanic ash
  and she cools

the brow of dawn appears
she sits
dawn extends

she is ready for self-control

*

Once
you turned to me

I prepared for an instant
of brilliance
the spreading ignition
of your lips

but a sour twist
had you speak instead
  of how sour is
    your   self

*

I was mortified
I knew you would break my heart
and you did

SHE WATCHES A MAN LATE AT NIGHT

She sits on the bare bed
thin gray blanket
she pulls at her breast
as if to feel the children pulling there
she lights a cigarette.
she lights and drags heavy

she's toothless
relaxing with a stocking round her head
Mannenberg
inside the flats

she plays with a baby and laughs
she throws the baby from side to side
and laughs

in the street dogs announce the late-night shuffle
of delinquent feet
she knows those feet
she stands at the window
looks down:

yellow Mannenberg
thin dogs
some oom out for a skyf

RECEIVER

Legs crossed
  she stands   ear pressed   lips pressed
  to the receiver
     and I   hot and dry behind her
dream of moist climactic peace

if only for a single night
the quenched being the only pure

if only for her steamy realm
her taut sweet kiss

if only for her lips to blow my horn
red ray of her tongue to mix my language -

then my eyes descend:

at her tips   two-toned stilettos
a blackened beggar in stinking rags
club-foot bare on the concrete
writhes in epileptic vision

but she (the beautiful one
looks neither at him
   nor me
ear pressed   lips pressed
   to the receiver

FOR VUKIN BEFORE YOUR BIRTH

To satisfy being made
for love and lovemaking
creators with muscle and bone
we have fashioned you
out of our seed-eruption

so every flower buds to blossom
and to brilliant sun-shine

now there is no inkling
how you will manifest our child
but with each turn in the belly
extolling the womb-universe
we caress you mutually
to combine and instill
the sap the spring the serene
future you will need to shape
for soon you will pierce the veil
of water to verify the air of earth

know child
we flank you now
and so long
as we have breath

WHAT ARE YOUR POLITICS?

Does the left hand feed the right?
the neck refuse to bend to kiss?
who is seduced when your figure
crosses a mirror?

boot on foot
treading the tarmac of an airfield
take off for gold mines in South America
plantations in Africa
sweatshops in China
a single question broadcast
on the airport sound-system:
> Comrade Consumer
> do you believe the propaganda
> about the end of equality?

riot and hot loins cause havoc
except to those who conquer
the river wears away the island-banks
overwhelmed
stalwarts rave against
avarice and rote
piety and reformation

at the political meeting
the great thinker and activist
suspended over the rim of his life
looks at those who make themselves fortunate:
living morality their ballast

later the body floats
glowing gold with dark birds
whispers
between adoring thrusts

NETTA

Older than when I
last knew her
she is betrayed
so agony has set
waves across her face
she beckons to me and we speak
she gives me a loaf
of blue bread
I break it in two
blue crystals
blue rice and bubbles
I ask if it is to be eaten
she looks at me
how crass I am!
this is the blue bread of eternity
nothing can keep crumbs
from coming together

THE TEST OF THE ENEMY

Bubbling from the depths of rock
untainted pool deep below the sand
I want to delight
you should not stem the flow
throttling the spout
take your boots from my throat
I want to sing with you
brother\sister
and water the desert

you see
        I do not want enemies!

*

sun wakes
puts me to sleep
the flow from below may instantly cease
   sun wakes   puts me to sleep

                yes death is
a necessary measure   a necessary pressure
    just and unjust locked in perpetual sad slaughter
    imposters to be unmasked   denied power

the enemy defines shadow
sharpens right from wrong
even as cynics ridicule and rubbish
the enemy provides the classic test
of courage and clarity

how humiliating when the enemy
    engineers a buy out!

COMRADE

I phoned wanting
to speak with you

to speak of what
I know not

just wanted to hear you
one who holds my head

just wanted to speak and hear you
here

OBSESSION

I   carry a whip
I   swear
I   make crude sounds
I   demand like a satyr

on my bed lies a woman
she gives me her body
   tantalises
pleasure's mine as I wish it
   plays a melody
     opens
and my phallus
   enters
and she ripples

   this woman
orgasmic altar onto whom I spurt
  my seed
I have her for my hands
as light unshades darkness
   wine and zol
   thicken the blood of rationalists
theoreticians of stupour
hidden from the eyes and the vision
strewn with bones
   charred thrills of my bellowing

all artifice\orifice   stoked with the memory
of exploding   imploding

SLINKY OR NOT

Slinky-slinky Venezuela
in her brown gown
to set off the green tawn of the iris
smiles Italian
lets tears trickle
moulding her hand
along his Greek-like torso
her man of honour
who will not deny
himself
will not betray her
though she feels
abandoned
when he flies off
to conduct meetings
in foreign cities
instead of slinking
into Venezuela

*

while the mouth of human
deadliness yawns
and the finger of human
scratching scales backs
and the eyes of human
blindness reveal their tawdry sentiment

slinky or not
she's full with him
and he with her
they lie together
on the crescent of a minaret

MERCY

No rain in sight
trees brittle and yellow grass
even as I come close
the mouse unmoving
whiskers quivering
on the stair
stupefied no doubt
by the red pellets in the plastic bag
on the kitchen floor

hygiene in the house
unpleasantness about
I try to sweep it
let rot on the grass
the mouse rolls
rigid

handle held high
I bring the broom down
bashing in
last twitch of nerves
it slithers under a carpet
I smash the broom down
to stamp out the pulse

merciful killer
administrator
of pain-
killer

WHILE IT THUNDERS

rain slits the city
sliding on highways
we drive in the wet past stunned buildings

before the drought
we prophesied struggle over land and shelter
-war of justice and war of locusts
now we reach home
drink red wine
rain slaps the window
the city crashes out our minds
another skid on the oily wet
hands clasped over the table
we are warm but vulnerable
the child in your stomach rolls and kicks
we name it
wait for thunder to boom beyond sleep

living in the war-zone
I have been forced
to spend many hours on the battle-field
growing the child in you
clearing space
(children bombarded from both
air land and from the water)

we agree: to be a warrior is
to face with courage
-encourage

ABIGAIL

Abigail on her bed in the cell-room
outside the honeysuckle and the house
beside the drain and the garden-shed
on the bed which is half the room and more
than half her life

she is radiant:
light flows from her eyes
from the source of the god
that feeds her

cheeks made sharp
she has bones that grow tight
we speak of her recovery
early discharge
from the cancer-ward

and her daughter who has a job sewing
in a sweat-shop on End Street
holds her hand
Abigail with the chemotherapy
deep in her marrow

and she who is filled with the certainty
of the blue sky and the white puffed clouds
of a rain-afternoon in summer
smiles at me who is so shaken
with doubt about each step
till I feel her light on my shoulders
lifting my far less fatal weight

DELIVERANCE

Outside the dorp in a tangled sunny kloof
they find the dagga field
beasts with hose-pipe tails
snarling at the sharp aroma
of spreading leaf

day and night under command
they slash to destroy the weed
heaping bonfires with bliss and paranoia
blue fumes at the tips of their moustaches
black plumes as the pyres flame
and harvest becomes a smoky bush

then on Sundays
raised high to the spire of the tomb
dominees pray for deliverance from dark
beasts sweating
uprooting their devils

HOW STILL HE WOULD LIE

Stiffly
he would refuse her

the dogs downstairs
barking at the shifting of trees.
he could not suffer her hands
when they crossed
but with his breath
at last steady
she would touch him
then herself -
hesitant bitter necessary
friction

how still he would lie
while she joined with herself

DREAM OF THE LOOMS

Streaked with dark and ache of hearts
split more than once by love
one behind the other along a path
the crowd journeys without speaking
no longer heated by the roar of the world

I see them dip
in and out of undulating sands
to stop at a great bank of cloud
then glide down overhanging strands
entwined ropes of fibre dangling

  down

      and   down   and

     down

they slide along the brown the red
the wine-yellow cascade of winter wool
    falling

till at last they stand
each of them at a loom:
two compact looms running
in a clean clear room
spruce and bare but for the machines

  the door opens

when the black hooded man enters
I am the first to cry out as I wake

    No!

SWAN OF LISBON

To the blue swan once black
as depth of diamond\coal
another song of Africa
where the howling wind
cannot douse the drum the tambourine
the lips of African women

you swan with neck bent wings clipped
have you lost your gliding magic?
say no say no say no
say: the blues are just a floating cloud
nothing is ever over ever complete
ever total ever recognizable from the outside

O swan swim from the White City
cross oceans
your wings oared feet
splaying splashing forward
greet me singing in a furnace
days burning to ash
as the hollow arm corrupts
and I gush my soul

come swan whom I met under cool vaulted arches
while ancient music played in timeless light
later at dusk gliding in a black canal
beside your fort high on a hill
I left my white canary
to sing for you while I was gone to Africa
and wishing to hear songs only of
Holy Battle in your White City
you came close and
we stood lips momentarily
brushing

    so I could feel the warmth
    of a fire I would never fully feel
    I would never hold you
    in the depth of night as one
    never embrace the free beating of your wings

now I sing another song of Africa
revolt raising it's flag over a seething city
the busyness of living underway
the business of buying and selling
and I send my other birds
over the desert and ocean
to embolden you

for I am still lit
by your kiss   your glittering grail

ROLLING

On quiet gray days
when trees hang listless
and the breeze that so often
lightens your window
is slack,
slight eddies come upon
the leaves like murmurs

what movement can cut through to the future?
what voice can call up the spirits of birth?
it may seem the only true growth is sleep

you lie down as bells and other music
chime along your legs
your thighs
warming your arms your curled hands
while outside
the street the buildings the trees
are only names you
dictate

you roll deeper

each muscle
ebbing into
dreamfulness

DOWNPOUR

Humid rain   afternoon in a steel city
body on a sidewalk
crying like an ape in a clearing
stuck with arrows
stuck with a need in the head
fumbling   hovering   vibrating
   slipping out onto the pavement

cover your eyes
refuse to feel what is seeping
out of that broken being
   walk on with your parcels
walk confirming the time for appointments
      walk the jammed city

it is hard to believe in an ape on the sidewalk
not only because the dice are cruel and malevolent
we throw and forget
that in passing we can still act
as heads shrink and go diving   we can still stop
   to comfort that trembling
our trembling
shadows in the street
      passing the crying

humid afternoon in a steel city
   hearts shrinking
hearts blinking in the passing

HE TAKES HER HAND

He takes her hand
feeling her skin shiver with static
and they walk like two manacled dancers
advancing across a stage
for the bouquet
they will take to the wings
and devour

DUNES

In summer he would drift to the dunes
watch sandpipers and the crest of waves
wind scatter sand like a farmer
then crooking his head
he would look up at the sky
-layered stations of cloud

and head rinsed with the drawl of waves
ocean sucking the hum of a trawler
he would roll in the sand
    wind swabbing his hair
layering his ears with the ground bones
       of sea-birds

he would roll in the summer
   in the dunes at the wind's whim

NIGHT OF THE ARABIAN DAGGER

You try the radio underwater
clog the filter in the pool
where your mother's orgies yellow eyes
you breathe the basement fumes as
the maid's husband
sings geroeked and dronk
you watch your father score another property
leave the paper image of his playmate
on the coffee-table
then you walk upstairs
shoot your spear-gun
in the bath
count bottles in the medicine-chest
switch labels
on that night when the volume
of Jung's archetypes
nailed above your bed
can no longer
keep you from fingering
the Arabian dagger

CASUALTIES

Under the glare of arcs
pale orderlies register the week-end stabbings
women raped with the knob of a kierrie
pensioners strangled behind vacant
veld in Retreat

once knives slash digestive tracts
obliterate memory and other nerves
rupture the vessels of this life
the victims lie cold
and porters wheel red stretchers
past plastic proteas in the waiting-rooms

all night invisible powerless
comforters move tearlessly
where dogs and chimpanzees
howl in stations of research

only the hooting of ambulances
encourages heart-beat
syringes infuse and withdraw
matrons swab trays
spin stainless machines

only a sea-wind sweeps the car-park
in the jammed wards not even morphine
can deaden the gangster's racket
he hugs a severed ear and swears

IN TIME OF ILLNESS

In bed
face wan and drawn
i sit beside you
and we lean towards each other and the feel
of your skin against mine
is so familiar and desired
i hold you

and the week away
disappears
coming back to you is
overpowering

this disease gives so much pain
must not be allowed to break
both of us
trying to survive our
human
life
searching out programs
for healing

sunset crosses the ward
unpeeling more and more basic
forms of energy

nurse comes
takes your blood pressure

she sees the unfinished jersey
who you are knitting for?
and you answer
and I say you've been taking your time
and the nurse says, men
and I realize I've been boorish
but it's too late

tomorrow I will fetch you
and despite the weakness in your body
we will tease out the longing
hoist each other into the flimsy
domain of pleasure

*

cold water in the carafe on the small table
filled with ice
nurse unwinds the rubber
your blood pressure low
but sufficient

outside dark purple
makes you cold
I cover your shoulders

I will fetch you tomorrow

you smile and kiss me
you know that
tonight my other lover will make time
intoxicate me
warm the bed and roast me

yes tonight I will make you poems
my love will be pure

MY FATHER ON HIS BACK/RACK

Body makes blood blisters
cancerous sores
eyes soft with dying
when my hand grasps your's and my voice
promises to remember the good you have done
carry the image of your face
retell your stories to the children

when my firm hand covers your skeletal hand
and presses it and I say,
I cannot go with you
but I am with you now
in these hours of subsidence
        hours of brutal disintegration
        hours of drifting
    hours of wondering at the blue day outside the sick room
        hours of final say

my father who is still on earth
open mouthed
    bloodied back
rack for the life oozing out of you
you were a good father
stood by me no matter
the matters I brought to the attention
of the authorities

you were an authority
 I sometimes recognized
    sometimes respected
 sometimes rejected

I saw you through a prism
strong and weak
a proud man
victim of the unscrupulous
   victim of your own anger

I will grieve you in ways I am only vaguely starting to
    appreciate
I will make allowances for your sometimes savage outbursts
I will want to remember the good about you
I hope to be truthful
father of the family
joined not just in blood and bone

it is time to give honour to the long lines of fathers
I hope my son too will say
father, you have done mostly good
you have stood for the good

I hope my son too will say
despite the narrow alleys
  the tight days
the gaps that threaten to escalate and panic
he follows a path of both our making

and so my dying father
here is my hand again
these are my words
to ease your blistering life and my own

SOLLY KHUBHEKA

Abandoned by his father
mother suffered a stroke but sort of recovered
he joined a gang
stole things from a cop's house
got three months, five years suspended
jail was hell
swore to never go back despite temptation:
break-in is easy

hung around
made a son
wants to stand by the boy but can't stand the mother
I mean why should a man
have to work for a queen before he can get at the honey?
got a job with a security company
danie fourie in middelburg
R700 a month to repossess houses

good at the job
plenty of time for karate adventures
solly hung in till fourie cut the wages
but back home in siyabusa
he was sick
a shack is no life
just days and nights waiting for honey
then sleeping when tv shows blondes
promises bucks
why not take a chance on the sun coast?

down in thekwini
moved around for weeks
looking this way and that
by the docks and at the Indian shops
but no luck
not even the faintest smell of good luck
and now on the road back
black bag
shoes round his neck
plastic bottle with water in his hand
he staggers:
please! please! give me a ride!
get me out!

solly's on the road back to siyabusa
theft is too easy
he hates jail
hates eating sleeping shitting in the same place
hates not being able to walk outside in the evening and follow a
woman
hates not being able to drink enough to get drunk
solly's on the road
please! please!

4x4 slows down
can you believe it?
solly can't believe it
stands like a moegoe
till he hears the hoots
solly slides into the seat
thank you, oh thank you, my brother!
mr cool steps on the gas
solly takes out his bible
checks a verse from Matthew:
'Tomorrow will look after itself,
Each day has its own struggle'

bible given to him by a coloured guy in durban
another break-in specialist
who broke his mother and father
solly reads to the man who gives him a ride
the book full of miracles
full of guys who have luck
solly reads and the man at the wheel
offers him a job at 5,000 bucks
offers solly a room in his house
offers him a cherrie
offers him free meals every evening
offers him a uniform and new shoes
offers him the chance to go home in style

solly reads from the bible and the man at the wheel
takes it all to heart
like jesus
you never know what's going to happen
when you hit the road
and start telling stories

ART MADE THESE POEMS SING

1. the brazen serpent
daphne taylor

In the Desert of False Belief and Action,
The Children Wander
So Long! so Long!
Where is the Promised Land?
And their Father, Himself once Pulled
From the River of Abandonment,
Cannot Keep them on the Path.

Time sends them Trials and Tricks,
Traps without Number;
Each a Darting, Twisting Snake
Whose Venom Turns and Burns their Blood,
A Poison that Blinds and Baffles,
Diverts all Hope and Education.

And Shedding Tears they Smart -
So long! so long! -
And Cry out to their Father:
Save us, Save us!
Defeat the Poison, Heal our Punctured Souls -
Provide Instruction!

So their Father, in the Tent where Night is Spent
On Desert Sands Quiet with Sleeping Birds,
Divines a Means -
He makes a Brazen Snake,
A Thing of Beauty and of Awe,
And sets one at each Child's Gate.

Come, my Children, Listen.
When Snakes Spit or Bite or Coil Tight,
Gaze upon your Gate and the Brazen Snake -
The Glowing Eyes that never Blink, Day or Night,
They will Draw the Stinging from the Soul,
Balming Eyes, Restoring Sight.

And the Children, Wandering in the Desert -
So long! so long! -
Clamour at each Word, and Answer:
We hear you, Father, the Path is clear -
When the Snakes of the Desert rise up and afflict us,
We will gaze upon your Brazen Snake.

And when the Snakes of the Desert -
Some Crawling from Crevices,
Some Suspended from the Thorns of Trees,
Some Idling in the Shallows of a Waterhole,
Some Hidden in Mountain Caves -
When the Snakes of the Desert Approach
The Children Gaze upon their Gates
And Reflect upon their Father's Brazen Snake.

And the Venom of the Desert turns to Honey,
The Coils of the Desert are thrown off,
Fangs that ripped the Flesh are bored blunt.
And the Children Rejoice -
So long! so long!

*

in the time that children wandered
and snakes afflicted them between the
mountain and the sea
on the sands of their desolate learning
they gazed upon the gates
and found their teacher's pitiless compassion

they did not flinch as the glowing eyes
of the brazen snake
joined father and mother
unity in mystery
unity of wisdom

they faced and laid aside temptation

2. business

manfred zylla

Imagine the dreams
of those who mined your gold
  imagine the dreams of those
who mined

imagine

the dreams of those who mined your gold
  imagine the dreams

    *

at first
you were open
  and relaxed despite
your shadow on the wall
  the sundial
  shafting flesh

you wore shades for
protection
and stood in the sun
with your pants on
  and made a golden tie
to drape round your shoulders
    a tie of golden threads
  many threads millions of
brilliant particles
    pure sun turned to shiny threads of
pleasure

you draped the tie
folding the glittering strands
  layer upon layer of threaded metal
  till the golden tie was knotted
round your throat
  throttling
denying you breath
till your golden glittering tie
streaked with red
  strangled you

and the shades you wore for protection
 defending your sight against
pure burning light
  fell and cracked   were smashed
beside a brick of treasure
  bric a brac   a golden block
laying upon a page   (torn from the book of deals)
on which was written:
imagine the dreams dreamt by those
who mined your gold

 imagine

3. Botha's baby
gavin younge

Babe leaves the breast
warm sweet milk streaming from mama
fountainous mama
babe taken from the breast
placed in a High Chair

time to chew
time to turn the cud
babe chair with straps and bars
high seat of judgement
High Chair from which to be fed
the broth of lovingkindness
the papa and vleis of hate
the rules of eating your neighbour alive
broth seasoned with gun droppings
stiff porridge for stiff necks

babe taken from the breast and strapped into a
High Chair

invasions/disqualifications/displacements/
psychophallic degradation

regime of forced feeding
lie after lie
till gut turns to gat
bread bakes fattened with boerewors
babe feeds and bites the bullet
mister botha's baby
ready to smile for the bullet

4. the dancing sisters
sidney khumalo

The sisters of love and joy
rabbis
drunk

tilt their legs sky way   high way
arch arms   a covenant
melody of constant labour

the sisters dance
giving birth to dance

5. the white wall on the hill
edward rowarth

On the hill above the city
square walls enclose a grave
the city, a blur of white squares
this grave place quiet
despite the swarm of ants and worms
city faint yet strong with light
a saint is buried in the mound
scavengers come to dissect him
come to pray on the hill
the bones of a holy man lie buried
four points join the white wall
high on the hill above the human colony
white wall squaring death
over which a palm
tree spreads its dates

6. untitled portrait (of a man)
gerard bhengu

Man . . .

the head, turbaned crown above
a blanketed chest,
below your wrinkled brow
cutting sticks follow your nose
anguished waves stretching, rolling across
your eyes, shifting . . .
    observing an angle?

eyes cannot look directly
at the bringer of news -
the daily roll, call of hard times, the ruts -
the groans . . .

your eyes   full

of sad anger

Man

    name unknown
or thrown away
    wonder
why   extinguished fire
hell of a lot in your eyes
the rack of time's trouble
    has no need of a title

let's just call you   a man among men

7. where II Kabbo was born

ii kabbo

bitterpits
is where I come from

there I was born
to feel the salt
of my mother's sweat
drip into the honeyed milk
she offered me
and the taste of my father's sweat
while he hunted the good things that
make us grow

bitterpits

deep in mud
where blood is shed
I pine for the moon to return
having only the sun is too much to bear
too much day without the tides
that ravel and
unravel

I wait for the moon
to turn back for me
that I may return to my place
that I may listen
to all the people's stories
when I visit them

ALONG THE PROMENADE

On the promenade by the ocean
under a blue/black sky and splotched moon
young people pass:

vigorous breathing bodies
stretching legs beside the white-foamed beach
while rescue workers help an Israeli girl
blown up on a bus in Jerusalem
and Palestinian medics try to save a baby
blasted by an Israeli helicopter strike in Gaza
and a 19 year old Kwa Mashu gang leader
wanted in connection with four murders
four attempted murders and dozens of hijackings
is arrested when detectives storm his hideout
and public outrage demands life imprisonment
for a man who indecently assaulted a year old baby
and two young girls in December last year

on the promenade by the ocean
beggars approach a man who is composing himself
this man asks the waitress for change
she gives him her hand
a busking musician strums and sings
young joggers offer their money:
"All I've ever had were songs of freedom"

SOMETIMES THE VEIL

Sometimes the veil fades slowly
Sometimes the veil slips
Sometimes the veil is ripped
in one motion

*

a wave forms
  swells
reaches its high point
then breaking
is followed by a lull
-a windy or calm surface
  rocking
the new tide rises and
another wave forms

*

a young man catches a fish
a small fish
he laughs excitedly
throws it back into the ocean
(it is too small to eat)
or tosses it into a can
to be used as bait
(he still dreams of a big fish)

*

Sometimes the veil yields to another veil
Sometimes the veil decides to unveil
Sometimes we cannot believe the veil
is a veil

Sometimes the veil is so beautiful
we insist on it

FOR ISABELLA
To the Memory of Isabella Motadinyane (1963-2003)

We came in the rain
to your mother's house
we found you on your back
in a small coffin
behind a thin curtain

three old women on a mattress
wrapped in black cloth and towels
men in the yard skinning a cow
entrails piled in a heap
like your poems stacked in books or on the stages
where you rode Coltrane's sunship
tight jeaned botsotsos
survivors
of the land of plenty
climbing aboard to join the refrain

the cow peers through the window
we drink tea, eat biscuits
the body of your work jiving in our memories

before death came
your friend tells us your tongue swelled
you couldn't eat
couldn't give voice
even for Nonhlanhla who was attacked
breaking your heart with her split pearls

now we sing to you
to the taxi topsy turvey
you caught on the corner of kerk and nugget
to the sweet shafts you sank
to the back pockets that need to be mended
to the three old women
on the mattress

we drink tea in the rain

BASKING ON TOP

Chameleons on the peak
green heads and gray tails
bodies rising and falling
hydraulic levers
on top of the mountain
-escapees from gardens

crows glide over the slopes and swoop
starlings nest   pigeons flutter over zigzagging flies

3 chameleons basking on the peak with sticky tongues
zap the sun
no wind disturbs the cloudless sky
ocean puckers with waves
rocks break from the seabed
become islands where water foams
and helicopters chopping spray rotate soundlessly

  chameleons
green heads   mossy craniums
silvery torsos
watch crows rocket dassies

    tongues and talons
limitless sky swallowing earth's eye

MANY YEARS FROM NOW

He caresses her cheek
she looks at him:
many years from now
we will be whole creatures
we will not live separate

she tells him this on their big bed
beneath the elephant cloth
tempo of rain increasing
music tranquil and delicate

she means:
we must always be together
without you I am incomplete
and so are you
don't you see this

you fool?

she kisses him:
tell me you love me and will never leave me

she holds him
and he kisses her

but still there's the road
the half-hidden balcony
the open sea and the open end

I BAKE FOR YOU

I telephone
to leave
on your answering
machine
honey cake baked
in my mouth

hot honey oven
hoping to feed

REMBRANDT

Having drunk from many cups
delicate discoloured hands rest sinewy
balding flat head/white beard
Amsterdam's rich coat flowing to his knees
soft purple trimmed with ermine

so many meals to shit out
succulence extracted from his own breast
the bland day's diet and the faces of masks
those he loved

he knows surface changes
waves urge the water
wind works the sand
he will not capitulate to the overload
furrowed
reserved
old man
reflecting

SOLITUDE

You return to
an island
ice floes and tropical suffocation
to involve
the world in itself
the days' flies
buzz about to die in the haze
love flares
so sweet you dream
of union
night descends again
cold but not
unwelcoming
you will lock with yourself
more rigorously
at times madness
flourishing
in the cell of your thoughts
and thundering trilling
stabbing song
waves of words
anger will wash you
living dissolution
if only you could wake
from illusion
no more or less
instantly
beyond
the swamp of lethargy and
defeat

TUESDAY, 3RD JANUARY

In the desert
light
subtle with the glow
of succulents

a cockroach scuttles across the sink
cooked vegetables stuck in the hole

I want to stand naked under the sun
echoing the call of birds

ALL PROPERTY IS THEFT

SOONER MURDER AN INFANT IN ITS CRADLE
THAN NURSE AN UNACTED DESIRE

I do the dishes
take out the rubbish
in the desert
light becomes so sharp the camels
squint

THE RICH GET RICHER
THE POOR GET POORER
EVERYONE GETS THEIR JUST DESERTS

A cockroach scuttles
I raise my arm

IN THE LIGHT OF DAY
NIGHT'S FOUL SINS
ARE WASHED AWAY

Drugs
Food
Certain organs

I dry the dishes
Stack them back in the cupboards

*

I want to stand naked under the sun
Feel no heat can reduce me to ashes
Feel the pleasures of heat
The pleasures of being on heat
The pleasures of pure flame
The pleasures of no name

The pleasure beyond perfection and pain

CHILDREN SCREAMING

A child screams

should I check or remain cosy?

I go outside

children fighting with sticks
chairs above their heads
shrieking spitting children

I call out for love
my neighbour in his garden stands watching

I call out for love
but when the blood breaks
I run back inside
find myself in the bathroom

a bandage on a mirror
doesn't heal the body

RETURNING FROM SWAZILAND

She walks into the house
pink\green explosion

he notices how tanned she is
though it rained
all the time she'd been cruising
with someone else's friends
who'd been laid back
but racist

they kiss at the door

since that instant
so many explosions
all kinds
of explosions

MOSSEL BAY MORNING

Red birds on the water
ocean fiery cool sparkle
spheres bobbing on liquid
dawn scintillation
provoking awe

red balls on the water
line of red skidding across the bay
slate cliffs phantoming a curve
we eat anchovette toast
arms hot with dazzle

red birds on the water
headlands shimmering
eyes sparkling
we salute each other
before diving

MAYIBUYE AFRICA

Let the sorrow of the world
not depress me
-neighbours with machetes
let the sorrow of the world
not obsess me
-neighbours raping neighbours

let the sorrow of the world
not impress me to the point
I forget the chrysalis opening
stretching out
to the greater womb

let the sorrow of the world
be felt by me
all the better to value the rain
all the better to love your lips
and the night that curls
silently in the warm bed when the music
is the beat of our being
despite the bloody nights of Rwanda

TO THE MEMORY OF THE 20 COSATU MEMBERS OF PARLIAMENT WHO PERISHED IN THE STRUGGLE AGAINST TEMPTATION AND GREED

1994

20 good men and women
tried and tested/forged in fire
standard bearers of the people's needs
and dreams
veterans of dispute and strike
mobilizers/organizers/negotiators
with
simple tastes – fish 'n chips, bread 'n coke
simple dress   – jeans, t-shirts, ragged jackets
simple offices – hard chairs, small desks, posters on the wall
simple cars   – dented jalopies

complex minds put to the service of the Common Good
whose uncommon powers - analytical/critical -
made a difference
working from dawn till dusk
in the cut and thrust of struggle

pansi poverty   pansi inequality
        pansi racism   pansi sexism

then the workers special congress grants a mandate:
leave us, go into the people's parliament
join hands with the comrades who fought beyond the borders
and on those soft seats put your hardened hands
speak out the resolutions we take
the demands we make of others and ourselves

2005

ah, twenty good men and women
how hungry you were
how hungry we still are

ANOTHER DAY IN RSA

Another day in RSA
eat your pap and eat your cake
it's make or break
secure your stake in RSA

shoot first, that's the safest way
or criminals will make you pay
it's old and new taking their overdue
the colour's green no matter the dream
take it quick and take it neat
be the wise guy on your street

that's the way we play
that's the major play
in RSA

RECORDING OF A DARK RURAL ANGEL

Listening to a recording of a woman speaking
   her poetry
rain falls out of a clear sky
train crosses a bridge
bees ball on a branch next to the gate
         swarming cone of themselves
   bee-cone buzzes and buzzes

early summer again

she remembers a dark angel who considers
tearing off wings
to boil down for rainclouds
-water for cracked mouths

another train passes
the storm blows out
hail on the ground expires
the bee-cone he once saw on a branch
of the tree by the gate
forms again

she reads her poem:
living for others until all can live
for themselves

who is this woman?
she puts her tongue round a man
thinks about the world incessantly
titles her poems: Conspiracy Theory

the dark angel comes back from the rural
hunched from living in huts
stuck on dry red dust

the dark angel swops wings for two flowing rivers
two buckets without holes

BURNING

sunLight on a car bonnet
reflection of Light shines
twittering like the music of birds
roosting in a bush
the child in his arms gurgling
beating time on his flank
drums and earth
Light strikes the metal
the man praises the star
Light in the burning bush

SING, DOLPHIN

Grey\white columns in the desert
I scan the horizon
chronicler of storms/eruptions of cloud
I take my bearings

I can cross this desert without a compass
but I can't bring my loves together

the telephone rings
my child says she misses me
she's at home with her mother and the tv
she's quiet as she speaks:
she hasn't made the swimming team
she isn't a dancer in the school concert
she's just a singer

she's battling with separation
she's learning what it takes to concentrate

she
my one constant
one

I say: sing like a dolphin

DRIZZLE AND SMOKE

by the braaiplace
you look out:

bay
railway line
houses
a hill

breathe in

hold

swim

breathe in

hold until you forget you need to breathe out

rock back on your heels

float

'cause if you don't breathe out
you can't breathe in

the space
between
drizzle and
smoke

the eye sees
what the pulse knows
the heart sees
while the eye pumps

then the eye unites

in is out:

be patient

WHAT COLOUR

For my mother a green
for my father a grey

both dying in their bedrooms
stood upright
in the lifts of the flats

undertakers polite and professional
quickly
wrapped the plastic
folded the blanket
hoisted the rolled up bodies

       onto the steel stretcher

I stood at the side   thinking:

how much joy will I bring to others
how many blunders still make   truths tell and fail to tell
      decomposed hours to clog my short time
      moments of gratitude

what colour my bodybag?

FLIGHT: SA 473

White cloud on a peak
thin cold air gathering accumulation
precious pitter patter

who can see ghosts between
the brown\green bottom
as the red slit fades?
solar explosions swung to the dark side
of Earth

wings surge

I think of
Ike's blind mother who
slept on a ragged blanket
by the stove
she stopped eating weeks ago
used to vomit up
except the soft pap he fed her
one hundred and one
misty blue eyes
skin wrinkled and rough
curled up on a blanket
she stopped breathing last night

I see next to me
the woman crying over supper
is the woman I once loved
who fucks other men
and cries with pleasure
this woman crying in the seat next to me
holds Fair Lady on her lap

ALL WHITES ARE RACISTS

All whites are racists
all blacks are defeatists
all blacks are victims of pasty whites
all whites are victims of chocolate delights
all men rape women
all women trap men
all politicians preach honey
all politicians eat money
all blacks live in shacks
all whites live in the Lord's mansion
all christians are infidels
all heathen wear slave bells
all imams preach mutilation
all women provoke provocation

all italians pant on heat
all jews and coolies practice deceit
all intellectuals are bored
all bankers like to hoard
all politicians promote their pensions
all journalists promote themselves
all the poor eat crumbs gladly
all the rich deserve to be rich
all gay men suck their thumbs
all women like it up the bum

all lines meet somewhere or other
all sisters need a brother
all brothers are motherfuckers
all mothers are cocksuckers
all rules are divinely inspired
all dictators should be honourably retired
all fashions find their favour
all causes find their saviours
all saviours bear their crosses
all survivors count the losses

'strue or false?

GREEN YEOVILLE

Ja, die hemel is 'n lekker spot
maar wat van aarde?

helter-skelter in Rockey Street
rubbish all randy in Raleigh Street
shrubs mangled in Cavendish Street
jacarandas jackrolled in Isipingo Street
roses deflowered in St George's Street
bougainvillea trashed in Hunter Street

weeds ground down with herbicide
pretty pansies spat upon
while they smile up at the god sun
ag, sies! wat makeer?
don't we want the Garden of Eden
to reappear?

all the cleaners in Africa
can't hose down the trash in Berea
shebeens attack the air with piss
vomit oozes onto sidewalks of grass
pavements littered with broken glass
heita heita
make your stand now not later
too late for tears when yeoville disappears
and archaeologists find
thousands of beer cans

TO ANNA BLOMMETJIE*
(after Kurt Schwitters, "Ana Blume")

Heita little goose of my twenty seven chameleons, i smaak yours
djy djou djou djoune, eke djouna, djy meine. we two skatties?
daai se proper plek (if youse get my drift) is nooit here, ou pal
wie is djy, unlobolaed medi?
djy sommer is - is youse you?
abantu tune you was around
laat hulle tune. daai ouens don't have the faintest clue about ding-
dong
topsy turvy touting taxi. you trampoline - that's how you make your
way
heita! djou rooi rok scissored wit
ruby i smaak, anna blommetjie, ruby i smaak djoune!
djy djou djou djoune, eke djoune, djy meine. we two skatties?
daai se proper plek (if you get my drift) is in die koue oog
ruby blommetjie, ruby anna blommetjie, wat tune die majita?
zama-zama bambanani: anna blommetjie is mal
                        anna blommetjie is rooi
                        watte kleur is die ballas?
ubuluhlaza wumbala wezinwele zakho aziphuzi
ruby is die bullseye van djou groen ballas
djou medi in sommer sommer gear, djou soet groen mamba, eke
smaak djoune
djy djou djou djoune, eke djoune, djy meine. we two skatties?
daai se proper plek (if youse get my drift) is in die vuurgat
anna blommetjie! anna, a-n-n-a, eke dribbel igama lakho
igama lakho dribbel soos sag kersie vet
you check, anna, you check nou?
mense can suss youse from the bum, en djou, djou most cool
djy is dieselfde - back to front: 'a-n-n-a'
kersie vet dribbel smooching my back
anna blommetjie, djy dribbelende mamba, eke smaak djoune!

*Inspiration from the Botsotso Jesters

WIMPY, HARRISMITH

Dry fields
fields turned to veld

*

4 young women in a welcoming row

I order chips

mothers bursting with fertility
powerful but trapped
by the flies
buzzing over the carcass of a township dog

I order
the women smile
good natured yet sour
they smile at me
and all other customers

take care not to be flirtatious

*

the only available table outside is dirty
smeared with tomato sauce and salt
I ask the woman at the cash register
if someone can please clean it

Emily is sent

Emily is a temporary cleaner
Emily cleans the surface of the table
in a few seconds
the table is no longer smeared and sticky

*

thank you Emily

KOOS AND THE FOREIGN MARXIST
New Year, 1987

Koos took the Foreign Marxist
to Hillbrow on New Year's Eve
But first they had a Drink in King George's Street
at Piet Crous's Sportsman's Bar
The Bar was bloody and full of Wit
Koos bought the Foreigner a double Brandy
They drank in Silence while the TV
showed a Storm of Fists
Then they trotted up the Hill
to admire the Shop Windows of
the Hillbrow Meat Festival
There were Shanks of Boeremeisie
and Strips of Pofadder Wors
Dik sections of Rump glistened on Hooks
and all the Punkies showed their Curves

The Foreign Marxist gaped in Awe
as they followed the Bikini Tops
the Short Sleeved Crowd
Men in powder-blue Leisure Suits
lounged against Ambulances
polishing Teargas Canisters

The Marxist stopped
Ja said Koos
Meet living examples of Dominating Intelligence
They advanced past the Barricades
into the Grey Areas of Pretorius Street
It was almost Midnight
Young South Africans prepared
to obliterate the Memory of a Memorable Year

The Marxist marveled at their Carefree Arms
They were Well-oiled and Bulging
Koos was shaking up a Bottle of Witblits
Commie he said don't let this Blow up in your Face
Here's to Peace and Love and Freedom

The Foreign Marxist watched as Young South Africans
broke Bottles over each other's Heads
Happy New Year! Happy New Year everybody!
Ja said Koos it's Time for your Flight.

ATTACK

Seconds after
gunshot careening through metal
iron rod cutting a swathe
to smash the back of his skull

she runs out of the house
stares at
screams
to see blood gushing from his
head
car keys still in his hand
night cold and cutting
windows of neighbouring flats
starting to show chinks of light

there at the gate
shaven man
two thick slick pumped up allies
falter
run empty handed to the getaway car

she throws open the gate
cradles her man
brain fluid washing the street
their children at the gate
crying

street light refusing to dim
ambulance shrieking its way
emergency signal burning the streets

she sleeps five nights in a chair
relieves the nurses
Dr Zero tells her the truth:
air seeped into the brain
there is high risk of infection

she prays to the powers
who fill the frame of love
and make her tenderness

spread over the fracture
and reach into her man's skull
to steady the throbbing

weeks later
under her banner
hands bearing wholesome food
raging subsides
her man survives
prepares to give again
prepares to give and receive
her and the precious ones
who make him whisper
a new song

he rises from the white bed
once again she hopes
once again she dares to trust
the world

WAKING UP WITH THE RAIN

Waking up with the rain
knowing there will be no work
he slides back under the blankets
the farmhouse and the dorp disappear
elastic drowsy warmth
slow spreading mouth
feeling her
before she touches
to make him
full

the thunder won't stop
rain won't let up
small flowers buttonhole the veld
after the sun comes through
after the heavens flick shut
their sluices

> In bed
> overhearing her breathing
> trains
> rivulets spiralling down gutters
>
> he opens and closes her
> two
> three
> four times

IN RUNNING AWAY I COME CLOSER

When the fist of my sense
of living comes to take me
away from your eyes and arms
when the broken song in my throat croaks
the song I mean to utter
for you when night eclipses
ripe day and the wholesale slaughter
of my too vivid visions makes me
turn away with tears
from your tears

when the longing in me for unmarked space
cramps the canvas you fill for me
oblong gestures in thick paint
a riddle to the flesh
we bear

then
I ride past fresh fields
seeking separate seeds and scent
mending the damage
making the moment whole
for you
my love whom I cannot
satisfy

WISH

At work
  Fatigue costs me the chance to prevent
fraud infecting
the hands who meet at the table
to divide up the riches of the earth
:
 the management of money defying
  Famine
  Spirit
Fear of Fortune
  Dustpools of Despair and then
Love
    when hands and heart and the realm of Mystery
      require solace

*

today is   thought and inspiration
 devotion to the plane at which
  life spans time
bridges the shifting of time

and I acknowledge sins
the ranking of perplexing weakness
(does this mean I have new
strength and wisdom?)

I mourn my rift with my daughter
it offends my love for her
this rift
having to see her
in patches
  in little snips

my wish is for my daughter
to be brave
with the bounty of human
invention and kindness

be well, my darling
live your own life

COSMOS

In the midst of
  the cosmos

    a sun-
    flower

crown of bush/spear of fire
  the rush on high

    thrust and embrace
  the way stars explode

cosmos
pink and blue heads waving between Heidelburg and Villiers

sunflower
  embedded with seeds

embedded with the eyes of travelers shooting
    through the cosmos

PHILIP

Philip is an electrician
his wife died five years ago
cancer of the throat

after he was retrenched
he lost their house
had to move in with his parents
after his wife died
he left their two kids
with his sister

no job since September last year
owes R15,000 to different creditors
owes back rent on the house
owes a lawyer in Randburg

Philip is looking for a job
-any electrical job

WAITING FOR NOMUSA

*

Waiting for nomusa
to tell her story
  drunken police father who
  used tradition
  to suppress women
her mother her sisters
herself

nine year old nomusa pissing outside the beehive
and cleaning up
-home lost

*

waiting at the Beach Hotel
for her to spill her bile
-humiliation

over and over it bursts out
again
the anguish and the anger
-cornered rat

after the great cock crowed
for his daughter
spilled his impulse
bare ripples on her ripe breasts
  mother left barren
  wrinkled unloving

he knows all about greasing
the truncheon
  big fat belly gorging itself
  cop who only dares
  abuse
his family

a working hero is something to be

*

the waiters in blue/green floral shirts
agree: this crime must be severely punished
and all other floutings of blood

(lightning does not always come
to burn and bring fresh growth

the welcome to durban
SIGN
red kitsch in sharkskin
speaks of nomusa's mother
-all mothers who hate and love
the prison of home
the poison of memory
injecting her days with gonorrhea
and black snails

and then he kissed her

*

where is nomusa?

he has a book on the table
-her chronicle of hard work
clean and cook
look after others

why feel shame when a marriage fails?

*

dreaming of a cheerful whore
to suck him bare
and feel her wet
while she strokes and draws him into
     her

       bliss
is wet rain scent
such happy words
while she bobs

rises and releases
  both of them
  mixed
for instants devoted to each other

meanwhile
        nomusa hunts for old/new stories
          sweeping up her eurolocks
-blonde nogal
curios beyond the balcony of the Beach Hotel blink
her cell voice grating
-tired after a day's humping
she sits in skintight jeans
sipping juice
while the surrounding tables watch him
letching her braids
her pert strutting
the heave of her blouse
slight waddle of her bum on high boots

she says she works in a condom factory
behind a desk
in the promotions department
what gives?

curls
cute as a kugel

yebo, siesie

  but her eyes have a look   sometimes
        that is real

honest   intelligent

yeah

*

he looks out from the balcony:
windscreens
rippling with rain
boats   spread across   the   skyline

waiting to berth
poets
lining the coast looking
out
for missiles and other contacts
-miracles

We never stole for the rich
We never stole for the poor
Like a curious child

no sign of nomusa

*

later

it's so quiet in these night streets
trees dripping with crystals
calm ships converging in the bay
aircraft banks over the Bluff
Groot Krokodil
sticking its muddy green snout
into the blue/gray Indian

*

next day
waiting for nomusa to surprise
him
-and she will:
honey eyes
brown as molten earth

A working class hero is something to be

sister survivor
sister to us all
sexy doll

Everytime I see my dick I see her cunt in my head

*

waiting for nomusa
a chill abandoned beachfront
faded lyrics and knives

if she does not come
there's the waitress with vinolia perfume
who knocks off at eleven

*

ha!
nomusa
crosses the road
slides into a car
whose driver is busy
drinking from a bottle and blocking traffic

he pulls off
as she uncrosses her legs

*

hours later
he reaches nomusa   cell to cell
she's sorry   she ran out
of calltime
she's at home in kwamashu
with boils on her legs and between her bum
-malign forces
but she will email

they will meet in March
when he returns to the parking lot near
addington hospital
smoke over the waves
and grace the tack
with his upright howl

*

his voice like the sea
how are your boils?
how was she yesterday?
in her tights
skimpy top
painted to please

nomusa at home on her back
just back from a job

*

weeks later

at the news café
let's see what happens
last night
she ignored his tango innuendo
the jazz

where's nomusa?

waiting for him to drive up and down
the windy rainy streets of umbilo
and find her?

*

still sadly waiting for nomusa

TALK

They had me on the floor
the stick came down down
they had me crawling and licking their boots
You can talk now
or you can talk later
but you'll talk
Ja, you'll talk and you'll talk
and you'll talk

in the morning the sun came up
(or
the sun came up and
it was morning)
they brought me a bowl of pap
coffee cigarettes
they said, You'll be a good boy

in the evening the sun went down
(or
the sun went down and
it was evening)
I was left alone for an hour
Take a piss, they said
get comfortable
tomorrow's another big day
Ja, you'll talk and you'll talk
and you'll talk

that night a spirit the colour of ants
came through the window
and we talked and we talked and we talked

RAGA RUSH

First rush of the morning
sky milky blue and foamy
demons with wings
fire breathing dragons
angels on horseback and the backs of yaks
angels so smooth they
ski down their slopes

first rush of the day
veins expand shedding the fagged tyrant
first raga of the morning and I sit
with the dogs in the yard
glossy fur sharp canines
so alert despite the yawning
laying out in the sun
and I let the first rush
take me to their tongues
feel the tingling coarseness
lick long across my palm

*

First rush of the evening
smoke of incense and leaf
day of mist and drizzle
air fresh as a forest
the dogs lie in
and around the kennel
bark as aeroplanes drone overhead
cloud swirls about the city

first rush of the evening star
winking
first raga of the evening
my woman in bed

THE EMPEROR

They took him from gambling
the green war tables
stripping his dress suit
they chained him
in a cell with crooked walls
dripping water
they shut the door and locked it

then counting the medals pinned to his chest
the wrinkles round his eyes and his penis
even the fresh wounds
spurting from teenage brides
they twisted his arm
till he whimpered
so much to tell of
diplomatic discussions at so many banquets

they bled him with hammers
denouncing his shrieks
yelps like hyenas
all of them foreign bank account numbers
then pointing his eyes
to the burning palace
he under hanging lights
plunderer with broken horns
they set his two goat-headed eyes
on the burning casino
the gaunt woman in her slashed sequins and tiara

they spat on his silver hair
news flashes all about
the provisional government

COFFEE IN TEL-AVIV

Mercilessly drunk
wedged between wars
I lay waste birds
with strong coloured wings
I ask for coffee:
make me bright as the sea wind
cutting canvas out the haze

galley chains slave-skeletons
triremes rusting with loot
in the kitchens Palestinians
salads for tourists
drowned Nazis and Philistines
bloating near Reading power station
another Fundamentalist stabs
the veil of Paradise

I want to swim now
float naked
beyond the breakwater

TEA AT THE DAMASCUS GATE

Cards fall from hands
dice roll from fingers
the only sight
a mirror shattered in the market-place

I sit near the money-changers
bakers' essence of bread
down the stony way
a green Border Patrol locks gates
rains rubber bullets as
rebel-flocks riot
glass shards reddening
a hundred spiked angles
shredding daylight power for the
insatiable ghosts of night
a hundred daggers glistening
with the blood of martyrs
cursing Jews swearing never to raise
children without muscles
for triggers

cards slip over dice
Border Patrols foul the Invisible Word
I sip mint tea
breathe donkey dung
a moment of peace before the next
bomb

CELEBRATING

you

and you and I

the sound of you
   when your voice
sometimes so proper sometimes
 so gay
   fills me with abundant lifegiving
      causes me to seek
         no cause

strong back and legs   toned and full
chosen words well chosen
because you have the knowing to make movements in space
  whole loaves   bowls of fruit
    gifts
spilling from your lips and thighs

you   I am so pleased to say
are postponing another
matter so I will be able
to hold your attention in more
   ways than one

      tonight

STAR PATTERN

I keep finding skulls
worn teeth
dry dust clogging red sockets
they lie in the yard
under my spade between
pumpkins and dagga bushes
tufts of onion

my mother here
an old stirrer of pots and hearts
sends me into the yard
to dig up lunch
sun burns my shoulders
she knows what she wants
and respects my discoveries

the skulls have rubbed sand
longer than we can guess
not even the old woman knows
how they came to our yard
but she stirs the pots
comes out with a prophecy
keeps stirring
while I go with my flock
for days and nights
into the mountains

I go and return only when
I feel to sit by her fire
stars embroidering
her shoulder her tongue
telling stories she can read
by the sparks in my eyes

BOY TALES
(ALL HYPED UP AT THE DINNER TABLE)

The noise level is too much
I slump to the table
he runs up and shouts in my ear
I smack him on the bum
put him to bed

he wants two stories
I offer one
Postman Pat's Foggy Day
he wants another story
I ask him to lie quietly in the dark
he lies back and smiles
Neville who has the cherub smile

I tell about the giants
who will one day live on Earth
very powerful men and women
who will lift whole trees
catch lightning in their hands
conduct it into their beings
I tell him how the giants will live in peace
with each other and other animals
they will sing and their songs will travel

he yawns
I suggest he cover himself with a blanket
the hooligan
my little boy
my dear little boy
my blikkie
my little seal
at last
ready to sleep
(my little wildebeest

THE PROTECTOR

He climbs the koppie
not hungry his lips a little dry
sun in his stomach
sinking into a donga horizon
evening lifts goat odour
a kraal's marble clustered dung

he looks at the land
stretching taut from his forehead
his palms his soles
over the mud river passing sluggish
under a railway bridge

he searches evening fires
pulls his earring
lays bones across
knife wounds of cattle and flood
bloody claws washed with milk
tail between his legs
fangs where he breathes the smoke
as birds scatter by the river
fly in a spearhead across the edge of light

the Protector in leopard skin
knows the idea and its flesh
the Protector knows that sacred
cannot be burnt in vain
he cuts his sandals loose
flings the leather high
they roll down his eyes and over the rocks
now he has no need to walk:
he is air

VLEIS

Fairylights strung from the stoep
kidneyshaped pool chlorine frangapani
spice of boerewors smoke in your hair
the pleats of your pantssuit
yielding like a salesgirl to salesmen
moving your lips your fingers
over his talk of 'The Market'

stilettos tapping partymusic on crazypaving
grinding a cigarettebutt into a smouldering potato
you looked up at the moon
passed the horns of his blonde moustache
that pale European - pockmarked but pure
listened for the world's turn
calibrated click in the clock
that outbreak of wrinkles and yawning
and forgot the coals white heat bristling with sauce

beersoaked and chopheavy he stained you
leaned on your slim breastbulging body
before toppling
breaking the rainbow surface of water
he cupped your chin
weighed greased you
that butcher
sole authorised cleaver of flesh

HOTEL IN STILFONTEIN

Brick bachelor beds
gold-dust in lucky packets
blank walls to guarantee the non-identity of dreamers
deadends of carpets trail to redburnt stoeps
beergarden's sprinkling of thorn spilling into
corridors of naphtalene and aftershave
drains blocked with samp and beans
concrete yards blinded by torn bras
the dining room's racks of toast shoulder
blue ringed plates offering frozen fish
chicken a la king with peas carrotcubes
blancmange shivering beside silver coffee pots and
packs of Texan

on nights before it rains
miners cross the street to watch floodlit cricketers
stumps are drawn
hail falls onto red blossomed trees

CHILDREN HAVE SO MUCH TIME
June 16

Confronting the bell and blackboard of
'necessary relations'
they break out and chant
march in their thousands
demanding

till the prisons are full
of chanting whimpering children
all dreaming
all burning with the muddy blue
state of

freedom

Necessary dreams

And what do they do when the soldiers come?

They hum in the dry grass along the railway lines

The veld is blackened after burning
the fields are yellow/brown
dry as drought

The children refuse the day's lie of light
they straighten the humps on their parents' backs
they scramble over the walls of their parents' eyes

They see the blackened veld quicken with snakes
and they know what to do when the soldiers come

They wait for the teargas

They have so much time

Children have so much time
they won't wait

GOYA

In the city
bulls gored and saints entombed
in sombre attitudes of penance
I give him my arm

old man
still straightbacked before the gallows
threading our way through a sewerous city

he shows me
palaces barracks shacks
streaked shirts
muddied flames
murdered throats

Francisco Goya
you mean much to those
who seek the special love:
wine gravy semen blood

in rancidless light
undimmed you live:
your colours
your eyes

LOVE COMES TO SHANTYTOWNS

In high heels
scent like a queen bathing
honey and petals
she comes to the shacks
by the side of the highway

she smiles to women
with scars and swollen stomachs
offers them
three meals
a room in the yard

and they leave their children
hovels where bones clog the doors
to drive out with Madam
having sold their breasts
their milk with it's ivory teeth

they drive out with Madam
clutching plastic bags with torn bras
then they hitch up their skirts
and scrub

WHITE IN THE EMBERS

The moon is full circled
shanked to a harness of stars
I cover you
luxuriate
on the sheets
under the blades of a fan

we have shivered
ridden into our frenzy

you smile now
half hooded
milk on your thighs

RIPPLE

In a garden/spacious greens
bright blue vault/grass high and low
the crackle of beetles/myriad microcosm
we spin and spin/crackle and zum

staccato floating waves/branch and stalk
thick and strong/eucalyptus crown
parapet on parapet/ menthol slope
sinuous slender showers/ leaf mingling
with vaporous blue/flecks of swallow
high as storks and cranes/ fluttering
with the bark and bleat/dogs and goats

rays playing/depth of space
lights our dark roll/ sweet smell
langouring/traversal of blade and stalk
on a flat rock/lizard basks

we lie in the ripple of the whirring

LISTENING TO A RECORDING OF VLADIMIR HOROWITZ

He performed in Moscow
after an exile of epochs
saturated with blood
and broken language

now that world either 'Jew-free'
or the Jewish world
paralyzed by diamonds and
black hats

Horowitz
merchant of rippling
maestro
precise lingerer

darkened stage overhung with organ tubes
white balconies ringing in the glow of lamps
shafts of light pierce purple bouquets
clustered before the keys

a blue dusk richly mute
with subtle fetching notes
tripping out beyond the inner
tempo of your tenderness

CRUISING

He looks at himself
in the mirror where he writes his words
in the steam
listens to the song
mournful ripple of a piano
reverberations of wind and a woman's labouring cry

then sinner slides towards the pit
where blood collects
looks in the mirror of his film
each character
an artist of deceit
sleight of hand and build

he looks at himself
the smooth surface
the polished surface that vibrates
with the slightest flicker of light

he looks at himself where he writes his words
plays out the whirling ways

gotta hang in
black bird   blue bird
stay with me
make me strong with song
find me a way to shine
like the surface

of the mirror

shine me

*

he's always been on the margins
too thick? too violent? too crooked?

he's always been on the margins
and that kind of life
is a bitch

so hard to take out the nails
hard to admit defeat
too hard when you also need soft

he looks at himself in the mirror
draws a razor across his rough cheeks
lets the hot water clean off
the scum

black bird   blue bird
make me strong

he sings because he loves to sing
      -essence is cruising

FELICIA

Felicia's wearing a brown dress and a wig that looks like a wig
-true
felicia's alone at 2am in the city hitching a ride
-true
felicia does not do sex
-false
felicia does not do sex for money
-false
felicia has a blank face
-true
felicia has smooth skin and big breasts
-true
felicia tells the man who stops for her that she's tired and is going home to sleep
-true and false
felicia gives him directions
-true
felicia tells the man she was visiting her sick mother
-true
felicia does not have a sick mother
-true
felicia says she must get up early for work
-true
felicia does not react when the man caresses her knee
-true
felicia listens while he tells her he's not looking for sex
-true
Felicia does not react when the man caresses her breasts
-true
felicia caresses his crotch
-true
felicia tells the man to pull over behind a truck
-true
felicia does not complain when the man drives on and pulls over behind a tree
-false
felicia looks around anxiously

-true
felicia asks the man if he likes dark places
-true
felicia is relieved when the man says no
-true
felicia makes the man hard and slips on a condom
-true
felicia climbs on top of the man
-true
felicia makes moaning sounds while she rocks him
-true
felicia comes as he comes
-false
felicia adjusts her wig as she slips off the condom
-true
felicia throws the condom out the window
-true
felicia tells the man to drive back to the truck
-true
felicia tells the man she lives in a house near the truck
-true
felicia jumps out of the car and runs
-true
the man checks his pockets to find his wallet is gone
-true
felicia runs and runs and runs
-true
felicia runs all the way home
-false
felicia is still running
-true

SEXUAL LONGINGS INSPIRED BY STANLEY CLARKE'S BASS GUITAR

Picking his ears
 dreams of
kaleidoscopic cunt
mount   the wiggle

   rocking
flipping   bass twang
that gummy bony
   feel

when the penis slides

this man snorting
 funk
he's on top of the fret
   the world is
 guitar-throb
surging!

DO NOT BE ANGRY

You should not be angry

I did not betray you
I did not bury you
I did not drown you
I did not smother you
in the blanket of another's
perfume

you should not be angry

I did not deny you
I did not surrender you
I did not exorsize you
I did not burn you
in the furnace of another's
embrace

please do not be angry
absence filled with your presence
place was your place
my eyes filled with our vision

when we meet be serene
I did not foreswear you
we who never were sundered

EXHIBITION OF WORK BY MARLENE DUMAS

Under the pale London sky
lambent clouds
I wander
in the galleries

the artist paints her Snow White
with a broken arm
naked tinted body
round but flat
on the morgue's surgical
table -
coal of cunt
in the valley of pendulant stomach
and thighs

sturdy woman with cropped
jet hair

and at the ledge facing the coffin
faces of bleak gnomes
who squint and fart
smeared noses
crusted faint eyes
small sharp bitter pupils
regarding the opulent
Snow White
in her tone of immortal
grey\azure
she who clutches a camera out of which
sprawl the shots of her life

sooty gnomes waiting
for the final pickings
for this Snow White to turn
to slush

*

I wonder how you would respond
to these paintings
without obvious frames these spaces
black marks and
white gaps for flesh

anguish made
brush

you who lives and demands
romance fidelity
soul marriage

how would you respond to these seizures
silenced stick limbs streaked faces these strangled features
you who denies the sovereignty of
spatter and dark
where rape runs
you deliberately track
soft words and smooth hands
that bring ease

you who cries when
I leave

I walk with these paintings
you whispering:
we will become
closer than ever
out of our wrenched bodies
make our love

IT IS LATE NOW

It is late now
crystal reflections
I'm untying my laces

the child is asleep
I uncover the blanket from her face
I uncover
unveiling such sweetness

past 12
night and the cold
catch at me saying,
dive under the blankets

I've been working -
writing and thinking
reading and thinking -
I'm tired now
ready to sleep
I'll sleep soundly
despite gun-shots or screams
easeful sleep will be my reward

NEW YORK, 18 AUGUST 1993

I'm sitting on Broadway
far from Katlehong's butchery
the fortress hostels with their desperate
bloodied abandoned men
in the regalia of ancient wardom

I'm enjoying a beer on this balmy afternoon
watching the West-siders erase
the stench of cordite and drying blood
the blocked drains and heads .

I'm sitting on Broadway in an Irish bar
and my heart is light
rain falls and the city slows
not so flash now after the furious
god Mammon has exacted his price
the American Empire
crooked with avaricious arms
a dulled gloss
more human now in the tarnished streets

I'm sitting on Broadway with the rain
drifting over the city
far from the hurricanes
howling in Florida and the Carolinas
far from the wretchedness of Katlehong

We should be generous
as easy as this rain
dark warm afternoon

PETEN, GUATEMALA

A man is buried to-day
in Sayaxche at this bend
of the Rio Passion
where ferries take petrol across
and maize and peanuts
pots pans and soap
tourists with hard currency

at this bend in the river
under the hawk's wing
the splash of the turtle
near the Mayan ruins cloaked by jungle
still red with the blood of sacrifice
the notary's son just thirty-three is buried

his coffin carried by six men
who knew him loved him perhaps
worked fished with him
played football and drank beer at sunset
while dark women braided

guitars strum in church
voices sing hymns to the nailed God
the God of the undergrowth
the dripping blue sky
this whole quarter of Sayaxche
leaves its tasks to walk
with the man who has died

here by this turn in the river
where little changes
little means much

RUINS

Wisp of tail in mist
blue wing in a fir tree
mustard cones on a pyramid mound
sapling sprouts on an altar

white tail
blue wing
mist
wisp of white dog

this world which forces gray waste
jaguars sprawled
with rotting meat in concrete cages
voices and purple shadows
infest a courtyard
step across now so vivid
overflow into this garden
sense of you imagined along my skin

Perfect morning for tears under the volcano

WE HELD BACK

We didn't get drunk
until the last few days
after time and the new
experience were beginning
to settle

in

we drank red wine
balloons flew overhead

but then on the white bed
we held back
from conception

SUNSET WHERE THE FERRIES CROSS

To travel the river
a barge with salt
passing from fire to fire

in the hushing light
shadows obliterate the day's
death squad

now this quiet
and burning life
this flaming subsidence
shifts earth to the west

*

Across the water
canoes cut from bank to bank
gun-shots
dogs barking
inside the thickening darkness
then your face
your door opening
wide

PENT UP PENTHOUSE

Across the sky
pink/purple/yellow haze

snake-ballon above the river
sky-scrapers
red blue and yellow floating
above green shrubs and grey cats

they sit with wine
loosening fingers   touching
where the balloon-snake twists

how can she be respected
when she is a thief of hearts
and pockets?
he says: become a keeper
not a criminal
trafficker in loss and surrogate

she steals only to return
double-fold to compensate
tries to restore time and those plucked things

lips loose with red
they kiss
when the balloons are high and away
almost gone

ON THE RIVER

On the river
passion hums
flows past the banks
the sun a silver breast
in the water
your blue smile lighting
dark vaporous cloud
as they make ridges

green greasy current
water laps at our tongues
even as the carcass
of a bloated cow drifts
across our kiss

TO REACH

She is now in a very far country
to reach her he needs
to cross a swollen river
the face of a cave
dark and mournful
he has to climb a summit
frosty and jagged

An iron ladder leads to the summit
to the source of the river
an iron ladder with thorns
wrapped round each rung
at the top of the ladder
an ogre from the past
stands with folded arms

He knows the ogre
he knows the river
the sweetness and the black depths of water
he knows the view from the summit
the dangers of each rung of the ladder
he knows
when he sets out to reach her

ENQUIRY

He was drunk
-he was with a Swiss woman

he was so drunk he lost his shoes
-he was treating me like a laaitie

he wanted to keep all the money
-he wanted to go to the casino

I gave him all the money
-he was with this girl in PE

he lost it in a shebeen
-he gave Stella a ride to Mossel Bay

he lost the money and went bevokked then denied it
-he never gave me all the money

he disappeared the next day
-he was treating me like a laaitie

he wouldn't say where he'd been
-he was lying around in the flat

he went drinking again with his chommies
-he said he would make up the money

he came back alone in the evening
-he went looking for Mario on Thursday night

he was so worked up you couldn't talk to him
-Mario phoned Cape Town looking for him

I thought of leaving he was so pathetic
-he said he got lucky in casinos

THE TEST OF TRUE UNDERSTANDING

Nothing tests understanding
more than Failure

tonight
I cannot sleep
my heart's giving way:
   relentless situations
      finally
   flooding my dykes

I cannot find a way forward
   to go back is impossible
   I don't want to go back
I want to be able to absorb this turmoil
   go beyond it
         manage to live through
            contradiction

the night is still with the movement of situations
the night is busy with unfoldings
I leave you in our bed
step out of the house into the yard
where the dogs sleep
under the rose bushes

the night is a paradise and a bed of nails
a room full of drunken men looking for whores
a room full of love as a mother and father
kiss their child
the night is dead snakes killed by poisoned rats
the night is butterflies shaking free their wings
amazing the wizened dealer

the night is you whom I love
and of whom I need to be freed

         while my heart shoots arrows
         you clutch them in the dark
         press them to your breasts

you press my hurt to your body
arrows pierce you
heart to heart

and I do not seem to be able to check
the black cloud and prevent it
from suffocating me
then I dump the blackness onto you
 because you have thrown me
                down
 onto the wet basement floor
 thrown more cold water over me
   left me to rot

                you see!
you see how confused I am about you!
you see me staggering in the road
looking for the glowing crown
image suddenly made flesh!
   queen! my mortal companion!
a mutual blood bath
 a mutual bath with scented crystals
when we hold each other

I cannot sleep tonight
 (the reasons well known to you)
     you want me
to be light and free
but my head
    makes my heart boil
      stomach full of cramping gasses
   wild mauling
unpeeling from the walls
     pages of other peoples' books

but I tell you this:
  one day
 I will breathe deeply
      burn out false desires -
      unattainable childish wishes of unformed beings

all will pass
you see?
I will no longer be thrown off my feet
my brain   a banyan tree
   spreading as far as time permits
the dogs in the garden
will hear roses open

Nothing tests understanding
more than Success

BLOCKED

Girl
  feels dead
    no sense of beauty
cannot speak   for herself
  blames others
is easily hurt   and hurts
cannot find the joy
of the world in the world
    hungers
  in her dreams
for hard and soft hands to smooth her skin
make her nipples erect

she has blackouts in busses
        is constipated
suffers   vaginismus

MARITZBURG BLUES

In search of Brown Street

the man who is chairperson
of the local pension fund:
where's all the money?
the workers are furious!
I'm side-tracked in the Bavaria Cafe
reading widow poets from Vosloorus
waiting for a toasted tuna mayonnaise
and a Coke

in search of Brown Street

waiting for the ANC election list to be announced
waiting for the Super 12 to start
waiting for the Metro Council to release its list of Bad Buildings
waiting for beauty to be revealed
in the corner of the waitress's
pimply mouth

in search of Brown Street

licking my wounds
licking my lips

A CLOUD PASSES

Spider reversing in a breeze
spider on wood
broken branch held by a vine
web dangles from the
half moon
half of the moon
lit by the sun
sun rays illuminate
a side of the moon
that half
rounding earth
side of the moon
darkens
spider branch turns
half moon blackens out

a cloud passes

the web returns
all white

AUTUMN: NEAR A SQUATTER CAMP

Hawk circles yellowed fields
sun shining pebbles
bakkies cresting hills
brown women sell plump bare breasts

seeing how others see
me

cattle motionless in yellowed fields
burnt stubble and berried trees
black road undulating over rivers
potholed by flooding rains

seeing and trying to offer love
to others

light blue the sky downed by hills
mossies spurt over telephone poles
wind sifts roadside grass
fires flare burning dryness

seeing
and sharply receiving

squatter camp behind her
white sun on red leaves
woman raises her skirt
lipstick smeared by passing trade

FESTIVAL OF WATER

At New Year hearing the bells
he stood in a garden
group of drunken Thais pouring water over him
high voices singing
drenching him
spirit of the masses making play

he broke into Xstacy
swallowed
half an hour stirring
head compact cruising
embracing the masses
drenching water fountains under the cherry blossoms
reviving rain

in the bar he found her
in this world of bars
lovemaking is slow   impossibly pelvic
the most desirable gymnast in the world
swaying
in time to the blossoms
water sliding
masses running in the streets
celebrating new joy
his joy

Bangkok   the place where it all came together

HOLOCAUST DAY
Before, During and After

Night seething with vitriol
-yesterday's foulness
yesterday's abandonment

day begins with last night's battle
our wills locking
breaking down Spirit

day is
infamous scorched graves
piles of shrunken bodies unearthed

today is memory of columns of skeletons
the final solution the final assault
commemoration of the breaking point

return from the breaking point

*

when I awoke
I tried to restrain my anger
tried to open myself to you

this morning when I awoke
car windows covered with frost
I could not overcome my anger

regarding the portrait of my mother's dead sisters
her younger brother
sole surviving images
three separate photographs
unified
part of my murdered family
whom I carry
in my breath
the bodies of my children

I scream:

    never forget!
  survive
dank misery of murder
  of slavery

*

when I awoke this morning
I listened for the birds

slept a little longer

dreamed:

a woman showed me hate
face set with the desire to kill me
I seized her neck and squeezed
hoping she would soften
show me some kindness
but she continued to shower her hate on me

I squeezed and squeezed
she refused to smile
I knew I had to kill her

I killed her

THE MANY FACES OF WHITEY

He wears a round straw hat on his shaven head
black track suit
on the back: Up the Bucks
buys 2 litre bottles of Castle
drinks them in taxis
speaks about the larneys who want to keep the masses out of
Sandton
says 'sharp' at least five times a sentence
clips on a Rasta Afrika brooch
likes to boogie to the saxaphone
knows how to break a pipe
when the wind howls on the Cape Flats
knows how to stir pap till its smooth and thick
when rain flattens shacks in Diepsloot

He carries two cellphones and five bank cards
can't take his eyes off the punkies whose black braids
turn Thembi into Priscilla and Thandi into Jane
can't take his hands off their bums and breasts
drinks at a shebeen in Fordsburg
eats hot curry
drinks at a shebeen in Meadowlands
passes out after a twelve hour session
car hijacked by tsotsis at a robot in Doornfontein
together with his platform shoes and leather jacket
applies for a job at the ministry of communication
writes a tv script about Kandar the African prince
who takes back the People's land

He smokes Winston
plays marabaraba and the lotto
calls every man, bra
wears black shades
reads the Sowetan and Business Day
buys a ticket to Luanda but doesn't fly
buys a ticket to London
sent back from London
forms an Empowerment company

buys a house next to a cabinet minister
becomes a financial adviser to the ruling party
has dinner with Madiba
drinks Johnny Walker with Alan Boesak
is present when Steven Cohen
shits on stage and calls that: Art
gets married to a pale woman
with a drug problem

He develops a drug problem
buys up old blocks of flats in Hillbrow
becomes a brothel keeper
buys a gun
bribes the cops
learns to play the guitar maskanda style
runs a nightclub in Rockey street
buys a holiday flat in Uvongo
becomes a dj at YFM
goes to raves disguised as a gymmer
drinks at Kippies
phones in to Radio Metro and bitches about the amakwerekere
taking our jobs
phones in to 702 and slams Hansie Cronjie
runs for president of the Young Black Achiever Club and loses
runs for chairperson of Old Eds Health and Raquet Club and wins
sends his step-daughter to a private school in Pofadder
dances with Adelaide Tambo at de Klerk's third wedding
to a Vietnamese ballet dancer
writes a novel about his experiences in exile
falls asleep during a Bafana Bafana semi-final against Togo
is threatened with deportation by Comrade Mbeki
for mispronouncing the word ' renaissance'

He is buried on a sunny Sunday morning
his funeral more organised than Joe Slovo's
more powerful than Chris Hani's
sadder than his mother's and father's

Rest in peace: Whitey

BOOTS

New York boots bought in Tennessee
ready for active heavy duty
in the metropolis of statues and junkbonds
ready to tramp the corridors of
Immortal Singers and their Promoters
taxiing the wellfed and freaks
past midnight through the backstreets
squashing milky condoms
as they fall from the lips
of blondewigged coaleyed whores
New York boots trampling
ice and pizza dough torn dollars
stubs from Kung Fu movies
ticker tape from the day before
the Stock Exchange went electronic

now

walking on Tsitsikamma earth
through streams stained brown
from palmiet reed bokkie droppings
clumps of baboon fur
stopping for 2 pink flowers
angelflesh on the track
air drifts
scent is wilderness
herbs red leaves forked
driftwood soothed to bald honey smoothness
echoes of whale talk and fins
spurting in a bay of acute blueness
trawlers glow at night
with eyebright lanterns to stun calamari
and a cloud of seagulls dive
into shoals of black thrashing fish

START TO MAKE SENSE

On top
(koppie's black boulders
    rounded
    immensely hard):

 sun sinks
light makes soft
 farmhouse smoke rises slowly
     into air

rock steady   strange and so painful
world smudged gray despite violent red spasms
estrangement often keener than closeness and joy
  magnify tenderness
sharpen and extend to the river
the horse mountain long established
rising love for the green land
black place of shining
space filled by suffusion

sun rolls away as we turn
 to build a temple on the ancient
 blackness

KEI-BROWN

Once you were cold
all you could talk about is how men misinterpret your looks
how they falsely negotiate your gap-tooth smile
how they imagine you care for them
enough to break other appointments
forgetting that your father
-he of the allocating class
buys you one white car after another
keeps his eye on your eye
sends you sweets and bread
while they (the men who watch you dance)
whisper during ballads of the love they bear

then he of narrow widening eyes
in yellow-red joined your whirl
a room of happy-go-lucky bilinguals
corporate or academic
all keen to fight the Struggle
he came near and made you warm
but you kept your distance
and lied though his hands seemed hot
enough to burn your knots

he declared:
I'll wait for you
don't care how long it takes
don't care how long the line
no matter how wide the doubt

I'll wait for you

so you pressed him close
the melody that of wine
and agreed you were for the oppressed
you swore to fight with him
at the burning tire and the gate
you pressed him close
till your heart seemed clear of cloudy vapour

*

The first time he waited for you while rain
swept past the curtain
drove down painting the window
with sharp empty longing

the second time he waited for you
he opened the door to let the drops in:
where in the city were you resting your head?
afterwards on the phone you laughed about
your week-end jol at the coast

the third time he waited for you
at the window while lightning flashed
and thunder drowned out his bitter question:
pitch up at your flat?
surprise you by knowing the number?
should I pull you by the hand before you float off
on your sky-ringing voice?

after the fourth time
he went to your door with keys in his hand
and nothing moved
his heart was level with it's light
nothing moved except the tips
of your fluttering kei-brown breasts

DESTINY

He travels
opens a fuller range of language
wears different coats
caresses immortal breasts
is trampled in the ranks of armies
but breathes imagination

then abandoned to devils
marks a nail in the bark
of a full healthy tree

over split seconds and lurching years

destiny: sailor
destiny: cattle/car thief
destiny: guitarist
destiny: archaeologist
destiny: director of orphanages
destiny: metaphysician
destiny: singer of savage and harmonious songs
destiny: beekeeper
        stumbler into fierce and tender, tragic loves

destiny: rising up . . .

RED MOON

After sunset
comes the yellow moon of early evening
comes the white moon of early morning
comes the ghost of vanished visitations
the crater within which lies buried
the secrets of change

and I am thankful for the food you prepare
the food you offer
I am thankful for the night
the day that passed in simple clear activity
I am thankful for the day that passed
in preparation

we watch the red moon and the yellow moon
and the white moon
then we turn to each other
and feast

KAROO COLLISION

Hawk tracking:

airborne
 abrupt
 shuddering
 house
 of bone
 fleeting
 habitation
feathered axis
 hovering
 spark
 in age
-less air
grace of primal
 slush
 spinning
 hoops
 shadow
 imprints
 on flatlands
 springbok grass
 and anthills

d
 r
 o
 p
 p
 i
 n
 g
shatt
 e

 r i
 ng

 into a
 win ds-c-r- e- e- n

ON THE ROAD FROM THE WILD COAST CASINO

Night sharpens the fragrance of coastal flowers
petals powdering button-holes
as the roll of the engine
the high pitch of revelation
becomes a rush of bright blood -
dead lamb in the road
severed wheel by wheel
past midnight in the arid zone
severed lamb glistening in our head-lights
fixed ancestral on the black between the markers

thus we render the lamb
in flight from whores and gamblers
generals of sated famished armies
the lamb cut car by car
vibrating in the blue\black
of the hemisphere with the bleating
flock dispersed on the road
clustering against
the head-lights sudden blinding
darkness

there is no moon no shepherd
rudderless flock bleating along the white lines
shocked under the coat of arid night
hills ringing a horse-shoe
fire flowing along the dongas chewing bitter shrubs
we gun past the lamb
as flame from its heart
spurts onto the highway and the head-lights
to feed the altar of our eyes

THE BALLAD OF LEWIS AND ELS

Check those waves
This night
These swells running
From the Island
To the Point
Though stars are bright but cold
Hearts are hot and bold
But first check the moon
The round pale moon
Here at the southern tip
A stone's throw
From where the ice-bergs dip

Ups and downs
Bass and treble notes
An interrupted dream
In which a sigh and a scream
Float
King Lewis the Dealer
Has a head
Full of worries
And Els
She's had her fill
Of Lewis' sorries

Lekker lekker night
Sweet with dagga
And brandy's delight
Rollers crash like the first
Big Bang
The moon's blank
A hand moves with a knife
No stone ever sank
Without first causing strife
Lewis' got his brain in fever
As for Els
What can possibly relieve her?

This lingering night

Full of blush
And the dice's bright flush
But who's the one to knock the blocks?
Who's the one to shit hot rocks?
Who's the one with mirror shades?
And who's the one walking slowly
Over their graves?

Ja, Lewis
They take you from behind
They do their job
A rival gang from Windermere
They pin you down
And shred your spear
Only Twenty-eight
But there's no denying
Fate
When you was a kid
You had it made
A leader in the township trade
The manne said
Watch your balls
Lewis is ready and steady
So sterk the devil's afraid

But tonight the twist is turned
King of White Pipes
Gets his fingers burned
Els has him by the hand
A casual stroll without precaution
They're talking of this and that
His affairs
Her last abortion
They're catching a breeze
On a shell-filled beach
Lewis sucks the juice from his peach

Ag, lovers are blind
Rivals
They nail him
They jab him like bees

Lewis shrieks
Drops to the sand
Els quakes on her knees
His guts spill
White like a mandrax pill
Then the Good Time Boys split
Who can deny
They made their hit?
They take off quick
And El is left untouched
Though her heart is sick!

There down by the sea
Where waves wash
And grey gulls soar
Els sobs
While Lewis lies
Victim of a deadly score

Blood on the Flats
On the Mountain
On the wind-blown Vlei
Blood on the children
Of the Khoi the Dutch
The Xhosa and the Javanese
Blood on the pine the protea
Port Jackson brought from overseas

It's almost dawn
Will he live or will he die?
Her heart breaks
As she hears him sigh
"Hey Baby
Make me warm
My head aches
Everything's gone crazy"

The moon withholds her light
Lewis shivers
Els bends as he clutches her tight
But listen!

She screams
Falls to her side
Poor Els
She writhes now
On the rising tide
She stood by Lewis
Ready to raise
An heir to his crown
Ja, Els was carrying his kid
But he's cut her down!

Her mouth foams with bloody drool
His gangster razor
From a deadly school
Put a stop to all her rigmaroles
Her doubts her fears
Her night patrols
Carrying his special bag
That mind-blowing smoke
Make no mistake
Lewis' fortune was no joke

A manic thrust
Fatal surprise
And she's dead on the rocks
In her womb forever still
The child formed
From their passion's will
Lewis couldn't stand to leave her
So it seems
Or did he hear
Double-cross in her screams?

Come close!
He strokes her hand
He's whispering
"I need you
Come with me, lovey
It's Lewis
Let me lick the red
From your lips"

Watch him wipe
A tear as it drips
On the Flats
On the Mountain
On the blue-green Bay
No one stirs though it's break

The phantom lovers
Are still by the sea
The moon strolls faint
Spray shoots to the sky
The southeaster rolls
Waves run high

Down by the southern tip
Bright stars fade
On the cold handle
Of the bloody blade
Mannenberg's candle
In Love's parade

IN LINE WITH LOVE

She had him hooked on the line of her words
spinning
beyond the bounds
defying the terms of realism
bewildering him
he slowly gives up
struggling to stop himself from
　　falling
　　　　in
　　　　　　love
with this woman
　　disrobing before him:

　her breasts -
one, full and round
　　the other, scarred   shriveled

　her thighs -
one, voluptuous and perfumed
　　the other, flaked   flabby

　　　　naked before him
　her words weaving love
　　　he listens to her
　　　　painful tarnishing of desires
　　the meltdown
　　　　　our lives crave

she opens up　　heart and soul
　　　then backs away
to leave a poem
　　da
　　　　n
　　　gling

LOSS AND GAIN, SCATTERING

Going through boxes of old
files documents articles memoranda pamphlets posters booklets
magazines minutes reports essays . . .
issues debated for years
reflected and resolved upon
but action

blunted

     thousands of faces emanated
into print:
    descriptions
     analysis
  chronicles of battles
actors identified in the drama of
  survival\enrichment

pages and pages of print. . .

    decisions: ignored
               submerged
               violated

Confucius said: Do not plant foretelling a harvest

why this fate?
philosophy still makes me wonder

THOUSANDS OF YEARS

We layed him in the tomb
cut out of soft rock
and placed spices in the shroud
to sweeten
the passage of worms

we wound the white robe tight
and dug deeper
so he could envelop
the earth he loved
sanctify the body of his Father

we dug deep so he could lie alone
then rolled a boulder against the mouth
and wept for our Master
wailing men and women
rolling a boulder the size of Sin

now we say:
rise Master
rise from death
we have prayed out of need
for a miracle
we are tired of crisis

SAVING WATER

Living in a heart with channels
arteries veins capillaries
purifying ruby running
day and night through all the seasons

living in the river of our struggle
tracing the sphere of stones
long smoothed by force of friction
strobe of lightning

living with rust and rats in shacks
sour mouths of wizened children
sucking at dried out dugs
furnace of parafin
gurgling in the throats of gunmen

living in the heart of pumping
the threats and treats
the honey and the sour pickle
the mix magnifying glass at noon
becoming spark becoming flame

living in fast motion
the deal the demon
living in slow time
the hard bud
the softening ripeness

living in a time
when water must be saved

Allan Kolski Horwitz was born in 1952 and grew up in Cape Town where he studied political philosophy and literature. He currently works for a social housing association and member-controlled provident fund in Johannesburg. He is the coordinator of the Botsotso Jesters and Botsotso Publishing. His first book of poems *Call from the Free State* was published in 1979. Substantial selections of his poetry have been included in *Essential Things* (COSAW, 1992) and *Throbbing Ink* (Timbila, 2003) as well as the various Botsotso publications. His fiction has been included in two collections, *Unity in Flight* (2001) and *Un/common Ground* (2002).

Printed in the United States
By Bookmasters